Encountering God through the Church

Encountering God through the Church

WADE RUTLAND HOWELL JR.

WIPF & STOCK · Eugene, Oregon

ENCOUNTERING GOD THROUGH THE CHURCH

Copyright © 2019 Wade Rutland Howell Jr. All rights reserved. Except for brief quotations in critical publications or reviews, no part of this book may be reproduced in any manner without prior written permission from the publisher. Write: Permissions, Wipf and Stock Publishers, 199 W. 8th Ave., Suite 3, Eugene, OR 97401.

Wipf & Stock
An Imprint of Wipf and Stock Publishers
199 W. 8th Ave., Suite 3
Eugene, OR 97401

www.wipfandstock.com

PAPERBACK ISBN: 978-1-5326-5801-3
HARDCOVER ISBN: 978-1-5326-5802-0
EBOOK ISBN: 978-1-5326-5804-4

Manufactured in the U.S.A.   FEBRUARY 20, 2019

Scriptures taken from the Holy Bible, New International Version®, NIV®. Copyright © 1973, 1978, 1984, 2011 by Biblica, Inc.™ Used by permission of Zondervan. All rights reserved worldwide. www.zondervan.com The "NIV" and "New International Version" are trademarks registered in the United States Patent and Trademark Office by Biblica, Inc.™

To the church, you brought me from a babe in Christ to mature in my faith. I pray you are edified with these words.

To the Triune God, everything I owe to you. May you be glorified in my feeble efforts.

Contents

Acknowledgements | viii
Introduction | ix

Chapter One: Christians Encountering God | 1
Chapter Two: Created for Relationship | 17
Chapter Three: Created with Needs | 62
Chapter Four: God's Relationship to Humanity | 78
Chapter Five: God's People | 96
Chapter Six: Encountering God through the Church | 111
Chapter Seven: Encountering God by Design | 129

Bibliography | 151

Acknowledgements

Friends and colleagues, past and present, thank you for the dialogue and debate that shaped these ideas.

Kevin Kirby, Dax Summerhill, James Roberts, and Patsy Dicks, thank you for your time and input. You have made this project better.

David, Bethany, and Moriah, thank you for your love and patience. I pray that you will be proud of your daddy.

Emily, the shade of my heart, you have blessed me in ways I cannot fully comprehend. Without your love and support, I would not be who I am.

Introduction

"Space, the final frontier." These words begin the introduction of the Star Trek television series and movies. From the start, viewers are drawn into an imagined universe with a simple phrase. A phrase sets the stage for everything else that will follow. From aliens and space travel to transporters and holograms, the opening words prepare the audience for the story. Another popular movie franchise, Star Wars, begins with "A long time ago in a galaxy far, far away." Like the former, this phrase prepares the audience for an entirely different story which is every bit as vivid and imaginative. As a fan, I understand that, for science fiction to work, the audience must buy into a world that is different from the actual world. The storyteller must build a bridge between the real world and the imagined world where the story lives. Opening words and phrases are often the bridge that takes the audience from reality into the imagined world of the storyteller.

Introductory ideas, phrases, and symbols connect the audience to the author. Words and ideas are shortcuts that set the stage for us every day. A familiar phrase or symbol can bring a myriad of ideas to mind. From marketing slogans to patriotic songs, our comprehension of the world is often populated with shortened words, phrases, and symbols, which point to other ideas, words, phrases, and experiences.

In America we are bombarded with slogans and catchphrases designed to evoke memories or feelings in an attempt to sell us products. If we hear the phrase "I'm Lovin' It" or "Have you had your break today?" we think of McDonald's. Marketing executives spent millions of dollars in advertising so make sure we associate McDonald's with these phrases. "They're Great!" and a cartoon tiger are used to sell cereal. Marketing professionals work hard to attach product recognition to simple phrases, sounds, or pictures. The efforts to market and brand products work well, and they drive much of the consumer business in the world.

Introduction

For Christians, certain words and phrases represent the Christian faith itself. One of these ancient expressions of Christian faith is the Apostle's Creed:

> I believe in God the Father, Almighty, Maker of heaven and earth: And in Jesus Christ, his only begotten Son, our Lord: Who was conceived by the Holy Ghost, born of the Virgin Mary: Suffered under Pontius Pilate; was crucified, dead and buried: He descended into hell: The third day he rose again from the dead: He ascended into heaven, and sits at the right hand of God the Father Almighty: From thence he shall come to judge the quick and the dead: I believe in the Holy Ghost: I believe in the holy catholic church: the communion of saints: The forgiveness of sins: The resurrection of the body: And the life everlasting. Amen.

Many Christians regularly recite this creed. It represents their faith, or at least a summation of their faith. These familiar words encapsulate existential and rational aspects of the Christian experience. Repetition reinforces experiences. When done in corporate worship, reading or hearing words like these draw people together in shared experience; They form new connections and build up a common faith.

Other phrases like "In the beginning," "It is finished," "I am," and "Alpha and Omega" also bring a host of ideas with them. From creation to salvation and from self-existence to sovereignty, these phrases represent aspects of Christian experience far beyond the simple meaning of the few words found in each.

A central concept within Christianity is that God has a relationship with his people. God's people encounter him, and encounters with God have lasting, even everlasting, consequences. Many Christian traditions, or denominations, believe that individuals are not genuine believers unless they have had a meaningful and personal encounter with God. Other denominations emphasize identification with the church instead of personal encounters with God, but Christianity requires humans to encounter God on some level.

Critics of Christianity often regard claims of encounters with God as anything from naïve emotionalism to misunderstanding. Some go as far to claim that people who report encounters with God are deliberate attempts at deception. Critics attack religious belief for a myriad of reasons, some legitimate and some not. Aside from the antagonists, others ask questions about claims Christians make when they speak of encountering God.

Introduction

Legitimate questions deserve legitimate answers, and as Christians, we should seek to have good reasons for what we believe. Christians are never told to have blind faith, only a childlike trust of Jesus.

I am confident that critics of Christianity can be answered and answered well. I also believe that if Christianity is false, then no amount of hoping that it is true will make it true. If there are significant, substantial questions that Christianity cannot answer, or cannot answer sufficiently, and if failing to answer those questions ends up meaning that Christianity can't be true, then we have a problem. No amount of faith in something false will make it true. I agree with the Apostle Paul: if Christianity is false, we should not believe it or preach it.

> But if it is preached that Christ has been raised from the dead, how can some of you say that there is no resurrection of the dead? If there is no resurrection of the dead, then not even Christ has been raised. And if Christ has not been raised, our preaching is useless and so is your faith. More than that, we are then found to be false witnesses about God, for we have testified about God that he raised Christ from the dead. But he did not raise him if in fact the dead are not raised. For if the dead are not raised, then Christ has not been raised either. And if Christ has not been raised, your faith is futile; you are still in your sins. Then those also who have fallen asleep in Christ are lost. If only for this life we have hope in Christ, we are of all people most to be pitied. (1 Cor 15:12–19)

Because I believe Christianity is true and because I think we need to answer legitimate questions about our faith, I will attempt to answer some of them. For Christians, I hope this section will give words to concepts you already accept. Perhaps I will bring up issues you had not considered. I hope to provide solutions to some of the criticisms leveled against Christianity about interaction with God. For those skeptical of Christian claims, I hope to provide a rational explanation of how God can be encountered and how humans can interact with God.

I don't expect to convince everyone who doubts. I hope to provide a sound, rational basis for the Christian claims about encountering God, given a Christian understanding of God, humanity, and the universe. In other words, I hope to present an internally coherent Christian view of encountering God.

After demonstrating the rational basis for an encounter with God, I will present a Christian theology of encountering God through his people, the church. My contention is that God primarily encounters the world through the church. I also contend that a responsibility of the church is the act of bringing people into contact with God through contact with his people as the church.

Chapter One

Christians Encountering God

CHRISTIANITY IS A RELIGION based on encounters. God created and interacted with his creation. God created humanity and had a relationship with his creatures. From Adam in the garden of Eden through to the Old Testament, the Bible depicts people encountering God. People experience different types of encounters. Some are direct, as in God speaking directly to Moses. Other encounters are indirect as messengers, supernatural or human, bring words from God. The Old Testament narratives are replete with people encountering God.

As the Old Testament ends, the New Testament brings a surprising change of events. People still encounter God in some of the same ways they did in the Old Testament, but Jesus puts a new twist on encountering God. God is now encountered as a human. People follow him, learn from him, and eat with him. Others despise and reject him.

After Pentecost, another new twist on the way people encountered God took place. God indwelled his people via the Holy Spirit, taking encountering God to a previously unknown level. The ability for people to encounter God is more immediate, direct, and permanent than ever before. Instead of God occasionally manifesting to people with a message, God is always present to his people. Instead of God being located in the Holy Land, followed by large bands of people hoping to get a glimpse of him or to touch his robe, he now indwells people, who then become temples.

The world began to change as God indwelled the church. Prior to the incarnation of Jesus, certain people encountered God and told others of their experience. People heard about God from people who had previously met him. While Jesus was walking the earth, some people were able to meet him in the flesh. Those people could then go and tell others about the encounter they had with God. When the Holy Spirit fell on the church, Christians were able to show God to people as they lived their lives. Christianity is no longer a report about a past experience, but a demonstration of a present experience.

While all of the encounters of God sound great, some problems arise. God is spirit. Spirit is not material, but humans are material beings (at least in part). How do we explain an encounter between a material human and a spiritual God? This is a question we will try to answer in the next section.

REQUIREMENTS TO HAVING AN ENCOUNTER WITH GOD

Having an encounter with God requires a few conditions to be met. First, the objects being encountered must be located in such a way that makes an encounter possible. Second, the person that will encounter the object must have the ability to perceive the object. Finally, the person that will encounter the object must take part in the encounter.

The first requirement for an encounter is location. A person encountering an object must be located in such a way that they are able to perceive the object. Perception may be direct or indirect[1], but having a connection to the object to be encountered is required.

To encounter another human, for example, would require some sort of access to that human. Normally we encounter other humans by being in the same place. We may be in the same room, or together in a general area. But with the advent of modern communication technology, we also may be able to encounter a person remotely via a combination of video and sound transmission. Video of an object is a more indirect way to perceive an object, and some aspects of perception are limited by video that may not be limited by being physically present to the object.

The ability to perceive the object is the second requirement. I could be present to an object, but may be unable to encounter it if I lacked the ability

---

1. Some will argue that we only perceive our own minds directly, and that even the physical world is perceived only indirectly through our bodies. Indirect perception is allowed since it may be the only way we perceive anything in the physical world. Indirect encounters may also involve other instruments beyond our bodies.

to perceive the object. My perceptive equipment must be sufficient for the task relative to the object to be perceived. In cases where perceptive equipment natural to me is lacking, alternative equipment may allow an encounter. In other words, if something is too small to be seen by my eyes, I may use a microscope. If a sound is too faint to be heard by my ears, I may use an amplifier. In this way, things beyond my natural ability to perceive may be perceived through the use of tools that expand my perceptive ability.

The third requirement to having an encounter is to participate in the encounter. I can choose not to encounter someone and simply observe. I can choose not to engage, not to respond, not to initiate action. In cases where I refuse to participate, I am simply observing. I realize that some may argue that observation is a type of encounter, and I will concede that it is. The way that I am conceiving of an encounter, however, is more than simply an observation. Although an observation may be a minimalist form of an encounter, for the purposes of this project a mere observation is not itself an encounter.

The three requirements will be considered the minimum needed in order to have an encounter. For humans to have the ability to encounter God, we will have to demonstrate how these requirements are met in relation to God.

WHERE IS GOD? GETTING INTO GOD'S PRESENCE

The first requirement for encountering God that we will examine is location. How is it that humans can come to the place where God is? Even the Psalmist asked who can ascend God's holy hill.

> Who may ascend the mountain of the Lord? Who may stand in his holy place? The one who has clean hands and a pure heart, who does not trust in an idol or swear by a false god. They will receive blessing from the Lord and vindication from God their Savior. (Ps 24:3–5)

Immanence and Transcendence

Christian theology teaches that God is in the world, or immanent. To say that God is immanent means that God is present to his creation all the time. God is always around. If I go outside, God is there. If I hide under the covers, God is there (Jer 23:24). Wherever I find myself, God is present in the place that I am. The requirement of being in the same place as God to encounter him is solved by the fact that God is present everywhere in his creation. Any place that we could be, God is there.

This is not to say that everything is God. The creation itself is not divine. God is present to the creation at each point. He is aware of what is happening and is able to assert his divine privilege as he sees fit at any time and at any place. Christianity is not pantheistic. Pantheism understands God as being the same thing as the universe. Christianity is theistic and understands God to be present in his creation, but distinct from his creation.

If God is present in his creation and humans are part of the creation, then it seems that we would be able to satisfy the first requirement of having an encounter. Christianity does not teach that God is only immanent, however, and a bit of a problem can arise from the next characteristic, or attribute, of God. God is also transcendent.

God is not contained in the created order, even though he is present in it. God is also beyond his creation. The teaching that God is beyond his creation, known as transcendence, makes the requirement of being in the same place as God more difficult. God is beyond the universe and humans are part of the universe. Humans are not able to transcend the universe as God does, so we can never encounter God outside of his creation. The transcendence of God limits the way in which humans encounter God. As part of God's created order, we encounter God in creation and sometimes through creation, but we can never encounter God apart from his creation, because we are part of it.

Jesus as a Human

Jesus became a man and dwelt among his people. In the incarnation, God took on humanity, flesh and bone, and walked alongside us. Jesus encountered other humans on a day-to-day basis. He ate, slept, walked, cried, suffered, and eventually died as a human. Because of his human nature, Jesus existed in a single location after the incarnation. Encounters with Jesus were limited by time and space, in the same way that other human encounters are limited by time and space.

Since God became a human in Christ, encounters people had with Jesus were like encounters with other humans. Jesus' family, disciples, and friends all would have met with him like any other person. Encountering

Jesus was easy for those who were there. His disciples certainly had time to get to know him. They had their lives shaped by his teaching and his presence. For people who desire to encounter Jesus after the resurrection and ascension, however, we have a different problem: he is not here. He is risen.

The problem is not insurmountable, but it is real. The most direct way available to Christians of encountering Jesus is through the Holy Spirit, which we will examine shortly. But we may also be able to encounter Jesus indirectly through other instruments. Those who knew Jesus and encountered him on earth told others about him and an oral tradition developed, which enabled further encounters by people who never met him. People indirectly encountered Jesus through other people who encountered him directly.

Taking it a step forward, the people who did not know Jesus directly but who found out about him from those who did, also shared their own encounters with Jesus. Others were able to encounter Jesus indirectly through their teaching. On and on the cycle continues, and new people encounter Jesus indirectly through others who have encountered Jesus indirectly. We typically call this group of people the church. The people in the church today have not encountered Jesus directly, like Peter and John did, but are instruments by which people encounter Jesus.

In addition to oral tradition and the face-to-face encounter with the church, some people wrote down encounters with Jesus in what are known as the Gospels. These writings were treasured by early Christians. They copied them and shared them with others. Throughout the centuries, we have had the text about encounters with Jesus preserved and passed on. Follow the chain back to the beginning and you end up with Jesus. The preserved encounters of Jesus passed on to us by previous generations of Christians are a conduit, or an instrument, that connects us through time and space back to Jesus.

Like any other instrument, we have limitations in encountering someone through text. Those who were actually with Jesus had a better encounter with him than we are able to have by reading their accounts. They would know how it felt to hug him. They would recognize the sound of this voice and the shape of his face. Certain experiences cannot be communicated well through the written word; however, we can have an encounter nonetheless.

Indwelling of the Holy Spirit

Another issue related to God's location is the indwelling of the Holy Spirit in Christians. The Bible teaches that believers are indwelt by the Holy Spirit. The spirit makes a believer's body a temple, and he takes up residence. This is different from God simply being present in the part of creation that is an individual's body, so indwelling is different from omnipresence, but it is somehow related to it. God is present to a Christian in a very personal way. He is directly present to the individual.

The first requirement for an encounter has been shown to be met. From this discussion, we find that humans can only be present with God in the universe, but anywhere in the universe is as good as any other place. In order to be directly present to the incarnated Jesus would mean being in the same temporal spatial location (place and time) as he is, but Christians can be present with him indirectly through the stories about him in the Bible. Christian teaching informs us that Christians are indwelt by the Holy Spirit and are always directly present to God. We can be where God is. Now we must ask, can we perceive God?

HUMAN ABILITY TO ENCOUNTER GOD

The second requirement for an encounter is to have the ability to perceive the object we are going to encounter. Do humans have the ability to encounter God? Can humans even be confident that we can encounter anything outside of ourselves?

Humans are amazing creatures. I understand why the Greeks saw mankind as the measure of all things. The beauty of the human body and the power of the human mind are astonishing. When compared to other creatures in the world, we are second to none. Greek thinkers were so confident in their ability that Archimedes claimed he could move the world if he had a lever long enough and a firm place to stand. Humanity is something to behold.

With all of our ability, we are not without limitation. Some of our limitations are quite evident. Dogs, mankind's trusted companion, hear and smell in ways that are much more acute than humans. We exploit this with dog whistles and use them to track and follow scents. Many animals are stronger than humans. A bull, a symbol of strength in the ancient world, is more powerful than a man. So is an elephant. Even a chimpanzee is about four times stronger than a human.

Yet humans are the dominant species on Earth. We have even ventured beyond our planet, and with advances may establish colonies beyond the Earth. In simple terms of accomplishment and advancement, humanity has no known equal.

From a Christian theological standpoint, humans are the apex of creation. We know of no other creature God created that bears his image. Humans have the unique place of being created in God's image. Although humans have limitations, God has made provision for humanity to encounter him.

Limitations of Human Perception (Direct)

Human perceptions are limited. Much of our world lies beyond our ability to perceive directly. We do not have the ability to directly perceive many things around us, on us, and even in us. I am going to define direct perception as follows:

> Humans directly perceive objects that provide noticeable stimulus to their sense organs and their own minds.

Some people will no doubt take issue with my definition. This is not the place to argue about whether information transmitted and mediated by our nervous system is direct or indirect perception. For my purposes, I am considering the sense organs as an extension of the human mind. In a way, the sense organs allow the mind to "touch" the external world. For those who disagree, my discussion on direct perception can simply be folded into indirect perception with little loss to my overall argument.

Noticeable Stimuli

For humans to perceive a stimulus, it must be noticeable by them. Many events happen around us that we don't notice. We actually experience much more than we perceive. We are regularly exposed to bacteria and other microscopic material. We come in contact with radiation from various sources and usually don't recognize it. From time to time, someone may even put a sign on our back that reads "kick me" without our noticing.

Moving beyond things that our sense organs are not equipped to detect, we also may have forms of stimuli that we have trained ourselves to ignore. Jewelry and clothing provide stimuli to the nervous system when they are in contact with our bodies, but after some time we no longer notice. The stimulus is still there, but we ignore it so that we can focus our attention on other things. Athletes in training learn to ignore certain type of fatigue so they can better concentrate on their workout.

Finally, there are noticeable stimuli. We are surrounded with noticeable stimuli. We react to it. We work to create it. Noticeable stimuli inform our actions and reactions as we navigate the world.

Sense Organs

Humans have an array of fairly impressive sense organs. We can see, smell, hear, taste, and feel things we touch. Our organs have parameters. Our sight is limited in the electromagnetic spectrum to a narrow band we call visible light. Our other senses are also limited. The fact that our senses are limited does not mean that they are not valuable, nor does it mean that they do not provide us with a wealth of information.

Limitation of human sense organs does mean that from time to time we must rely on other instruments to allow us to perceive events. Use of a microscope or telescope allows us to see things that we might not be able to see without them. Our sense organs work with a good degree of reliability. While some skeptics might argue that we lack certainty about the things we experience in the real world, few doubt the reliability of human senses to experience the world. This project will proceed accepting the idea that human sense perceptions are generally reliable, although limited.

Mind

The mind of a human is capable of tremendous feats. It absorbs constant input from the senses and processes that input to help us make sense of the world. In addition, our minds have conceived of wonderful beauty and figured out some mysterious aspects of the universe. From the time we begin learning as a child until we die, our minds allow us to direct our interaction with the world.

Our own thoughts may be some of the only things we perceive directly. Whether or not perceptions from our sense organs are direct or indirect, perceptions of our own minds are certainly direct. Access to our own minds have also been thought to be privileged. In other words, no one else can perceive our thoughts. While some advances in technology are beginning to challenge that idea, at this point we will proceed with the idea that human thoughts are privileged. In the future, the conception that human thoughts are privileged may be challenged with new technological developments, but not now.

Limitations of Human Perceptions (Indirect)

Humans lack the ability to perceive directly much of reality. Where we have a lack of natural ability, we employ other objects as instruments of perception. Instruments of perception can take many forms and have varying degrees of reliability. For the purpose of this project, I will define indirect perception as follows:

> Humans indirectly perceive objects by directly perceiving other objects that serve as a conduit between the object being indirectly perceived and the human.

All human perception will be indirect in the sense that the mind is ultimately doing the perceiving. The mind is receiving stimuli either from the sense organs or from itself. Much of what humans perceive is mediated through other objects. Humans directly perceive objects that their sense organs are able to process. Humans indirectly perceive objects by directly perceiving other objects.

For example, I walk into my garden and find a hole filled with water. I cannot see through the water, so I'm unable to determine the dimensions of the hole. If the hole was empty, I could visually inspect it (or perceive it with my eyes). Since the hole is filled with muddy water, I have the option of sticking my hand or foot in the hole in order to perceive the dimensions of the hole.

I also have the option of using another object, or instrument, to examine the hole. In this case, let's say I grab a stick. I use the stick to probe the depth and dimensions of the hole. I am directly perceiving the stick. As I place the stick in the hole and move it around, I perceive the hole indirectly by my direct perception of the stick.

We use tools to help us perceive things we cannot perceive without them or to have more accurate assessments of the things we perceive. We use gauges to inform us of fuel levels, pressure in a tank, or speed. We use thermometers for temperature. The kinds of tools we use to perceive the world are nearly limitless.

Reliability of the Senses

I trust the input that I receive to varying degrees. Sometimes I am very confident in the sensory input I receive. When I am outside in the winter and I feel cold, I have very little doubt that I am experiencing cold. When I look out a window and observe a tree, I normally do not doubt that my eyes are sending good stimuli to my brain. Our sense organs are generally reliable in providing our minds with correct input. While they are good, they are not perfect, and sometimes they fail. Our senses sometimes become impaired by accident, disease, age, or other conditions.

When I know or suspect that my sense organs may not be as reliable, I do not trust them as much as when I am confident they are providing accurate information. In the same way, when I use an instrument to perceive an object, I trust it to the degree that I believe it is providing reliable readings. When I have to tap a gauge to get it to move, I trust it less than one that works smoothly. I trust properly calibrated thermometers more than I trust old thermometers that appear damaged. We make judgment calls about the reliability of our own senses and of the instruments we use.

Another issue is proper interpretation of our sense input. Sometimes we have good sensory input, but we make bad decisions about what we are actually perceiving. At night, sometimes we might wake and see shadows in our room that resemble an intruder, and we may react as if an intruder were in our room. We might hear a noise from a paper rustling in the breeze of the fan and think a mouse is crawling on our floor.

In cases like this, we have been provided with good input from the senses, but we made errors in properly assessing the information. Numerous reasons may explain why we made poor assessment of the stimulus, but we must be willing to admit that we are not always perfect in assessing the sense input we receive.

Divine Initiative Overcomes Human Limitations

For all of our imperfections, and all of our limitations, we are not hopeless. God knew what we would be able to perceive without aid and with the use of tools. Because we believe that God created us in his image and for the purpose of performing functions in this world, we have a good basis for believing that God made us capable of perceiving this world with some degree of accuracy.

If we were designed for this world, we should expect that God would make us suitable for this world. God has given humanity dominion over the world, and he has also given humanity the ability to perceive the world in order to exercise said dominion. God expects us to make judgments, to do right, and to represent him in the world. He has given us the proper sense organs to allow us to experience the world with a degree of reliability that will allow us to make judgments, to do right, and to function as his representatives.

Humanity has limitations. The limitations are not such that they render us unable to function. God has designed both the world and the creatures in the world so that they can function according to his purposes. A requirement of functioning according to God's purposes is that we perceive the world with a degree of precision and reliability suitable to the tasks God has called us to perform. As Christians, we can be confident in our ability to apprehend the world and make sense of it because of the design of the creation and the mandates he has placed upon humans.

With all of our limitations, humans have the ability to perceive God. The ability to encounter God is rooted in the way we were designed by God. God intended to have a relationship with humanity, and humans are designed in such a way that we can perceive God. We perceive God through the created order (even inanimate objects testify to the glory of God), through his direct actions with humanity. Humanity has the ability to encounter God because God created humanity for the purpose of encountering himself.

ACTING IN THE ENCOUNTER

We have determined that we can be in a suitable location to encounter God and that humanity is equipped for the task of encountering God. With two of the three requirements satisfied, we will now examine the final requirement for encountering God, the ability to participate in the encounter. Why should we think that we would be able to encounter God who is transcendent? The difference between God and humanity is greater than the difference between humanity and simple bacteria. It would be presumptuous for bacteria to think it was capable of communication with humans. Why is it different for humans to communicate with God?

When we look at the problem in terms of degrees of difference, we can see why some might doubt that we can communicate with God. Even if bacteria were able to have the capability to communicate with humanity, what guarantee would there be that humans would be interested in responding to the bacteria? Why would humans have very much interest in what bacteria might wish to communicate? If bacteria were to make requests from humans like we make requests from God, why would we want to respond? Would bacteria ask things of humans like the following:

> Oh great human, please give us food scraps to live on, shade us from direct sunlight, and deliver us from bleach.

I venture to guess that humans would not take much interest in the requests of bacteria, even if they had the capability to communicate with us.

So why do we think that God is interested in communication from humans? We believe that God is interested in communicating with us because he called us to be in relationship with himself. For his own reasons, God wants to communicate with humans. Since God desires to communicate with us, he overcomes our limitations to allow us to communicate with him. God comes down to our level (God condescends) so that we can understand him and respond to him. God would be able to understand us without coming to our level, but we would be unable to understand him if he did not communicate within the finite ability humans have to understand things. God calls us and overcomes our limitations, but he allows us to respond to his calling or to turn away from his calling. He does not force us to be in relationship with him. God permits the divine-human relationship and initiates the divine-human relationship, but he allows humans to respond to his offer of the divine-human relationship in a positive (accepting) manner and a negative (rejecting) manner.

GOD CALLS PEOPLE TO HIMSELF

Old Testament

From the creation of the first humans, God granted humans opportunity to have a relationship with him. Throughout the Old Testament, God brought people into a relationship with himself. This happens with Adam and then

Eve. The Bible pictures them walking with God in the garden and receiving instructions about their lives. Even after the fall, God makes clothes for the couple and communicates with their children.

God is shown as active in the relationship between certain humans and himself. God calls Abram to leave his family and travel to a new land. Later he visits and tells him that he will be a father to a vast number of descendants. God enters into a covenant with him and tests him by ordering him to sacrifice his son. Abram, later Abraham, is called a friend of God.

Jacob also encountered God and wrestled with him until he was blessed. Joseph interpreted dreams with God's assistance and was blessed in Egypt because God was with him. Moses was called to the mountain by God and led the Israelites out of Egypt while following God's leading. Over and over again we see God having a relationship with individuals in the Old Testament.

Going beyond individual relationships, we also see God entering into a relationship with a people. As a nation, Israel is called to be in relationship with God. God provides written instructions and a proper method of worship for his people to maintain a relationship with him.

The Old Testament has instructions for different aspects of life. God provided instructions for the community, proper conduct between people, family conduct, and religious practice. For example, in Deuteronomy 24, God forbade taking millstones to secure a debt. Lending practices were, to some degree, regulated by God. The twenty-first chapter of Deuteronomy has regulations for inheritance when there is family conflict. Finally, the first chapter of Leviticus has regulations for the quality of an animal to be used for a burnt offering. Along with many other regulations, God provided guidance for the Israelites so that they, as a nation, could be in a proper relationship with him.

God used judgment to confirm his relationship with his people. When Israel drifted from God and abused the relationship, God reminded them of their disobedience through judgment. Prophets called for repentance, and the people ignored the message. Eventually, God acted by judging his people so that they would return to a proper relationship with him.

In 1 Samuel, the Israelites lose the ark of the covenant as a result of the nation's failure to be faithful to God. The Israelites turned back to God after losing the ark and suffering military defeat. Likewise, the unfaithfulness that led to the Babylonian exile eventually saw God's people repent and turn back to him.

New Testament

The New Testament provides a new way of God calling people into a relationship with himself. Instead of calling a single people to be in relationship with him, he calls all people to be in relationship with him in his church. The church breaks racial and cultural boundaries in a way that Israel never did. God called the church to take the opportunity for relationship with God to all peoples. Instead of God having a relationship with one nation, through the church, God will have relationships with all nations.

The radical message of God, allowing all nations to be in relationship with him, continues the pattern we see of God expanding the scope of those he calls into relationship with himself. God began allowing specific people to be in relationship with him, starting with Adam. He allowed families and tribes to be in relationship with him over time. He allowed a single nation of people to be in relationship with him. Each time, more mercy and grace are displayed to the world as God offers more and more people the privilege of knowing him. Through the establishment of the church, God calls all nations, peoples, tribes, and tongues to be in relationship with him.

This is a beautiful example of God giving more and more of himself to his creation, as more and more of his creatures enter into relationship with him and are adopted into his family. Through time, God's love has unfolded to ever greater numbers of people. More and more humans have been invited to partake of the riches of the divine inheritance in the church as each year has passed. God has delayed the return of Christ as a merciful and gracious act, allowing more and more people the opportunity to know him. In Matthew 13:31–32, Jesus tells his disciples:

> He told them another parable: "The kingdom of heaven is like a mustard seed, which a man took and planted in his field. Though it is the smallest of all seeds, yet when it grows, it is the largest of garden plants and becomes a tree, so that the birds come and perch in its branches."

When Jesus used the parable of the mustard seed to depict the kingdom of God, it grew from very small to immensely large. God's love for humans and his offer of a relationship with himself to them can be seen as expanding like the mustard seed.

GOD OVERCOMES HUMAN LIMITATIONS ENABLING RESPONSE

God's offer of a relationship has been ever expanding and shows a greater and greater outpouring of his love. Given human limitations, we would have been unable to know about God or respond to him except that he overcomes our limitations so that we could respond to him.

God's ways are higher than our ways. God's thoughts are higher than our thoughts. God graciously condescends to a level that humans can understand. He communicates with us in language and concepts we can understand. God uses analogies so we can grasp meaning. God uses dreams, visions, and pictures in ways that allow humans to know his will. If God did not choose to communicate with us so that we could understand and respond to his leading, we would be lost. We would have no hope of a relationship with God.

God begins and enables communication with humanity. We can respond to God only because he initiated the communication. We can understand God only because he descends to our level. We have a role to play in communicating with God, but we should not forget that our role is completely dependent on God. From start to finish, God is required.

HUMANS RESPOND TO GOD'S CALL POSITIVELY OR NEGATIVELY

God has called people to be in relationship with him and he has overcome human limitations so that we can be in relationship with him. Now, at the end, after God has done so much to enable the relationship with humanity, we have to respond to God's call. The relationship God offers is that of a loving Creator and father to a creature and heir. God created everything other than himself. We are among the created order. We stand in relationship to God as a creature to the Creator. God offers us the opportunity to have another type of relationship to him also. He offers to adopt us into his family and to have the relationship of a father to a child (heir).

The first relationship with God, creature to Creator, was set from the moment of creation. We don't have to encounter God to stand in this relationship. Simply put, we are his creatures, and he is the Creator. We can't opt out of this relationship.

The second relationship is a filial one, mutually loving. God offers to love us and to allow us to love him. God offers to right the wrongs we have done, and to give us an inheritance of an heir. This offer, however, is not automatic. This relationship requires an encounter with God in which we respond in love to his offer of love. This offer requires us to accept God's love for us and offer our own love to him. We must respond positively, turn toward God's call, to be in a filial relationship with him.

If we don't want to accept this offer, we can refuse. God does not force us into a filial relationship with him. We can respond negatively, turning away from God's call. If we do so, we remain outside of the family and only relate to God as creature to Creator.

CONCLUSION

Although transcendent, God is accessible to humanity. Humans have the ability to encounter him because he overcame human limitations by revealing himself. God has enabled people to respond to his call for relationship and salvation.

This chapter has set the groundwork for the rest of the book. God can be encountered by humans. God, on his own initiative, has ordered creation so that humanity may encounter him. God lovingly and graciously calls us to encounter him. He enables us to be in relationship with himself. He overcomes our limitations and comes down to our level.

Having demonstrated how humanity can encounter God, in the remainder of the book I will set out to show how human purpose is fulfilled in a relationship with God. I will demonstrate the way that the purpose of humanity is found in God's plan. I will also show that humans are created with needs, and that those needs are met in relationship with God. Then I will show that the primary way God is encountered is through his people, the church. Finally, I will demonstrate why attempts to encounter God apart from his church are deficient.

Chapter Two

Created for Relationship

> How many are your works, Lord! In wisdom you made them all;
> the earth is full of your creatures. (Ps 104:24)

DISCUSSION OF HUMAN ORIGINS can be filled with passion. In some circles, it is plain as day that humans, along with all other life on earth, came from a common ancestor. Biological and geological evidence undergird the claim that sometime in the distant past a simple life form emerged on this planet and, over the millennia, unguided mutation brought forth species that resulted in humanity.

The passionate part of the discussion may come into play when someone who takes a different view of human origins suggests another option. When a religious person suggests that the originator of all life on the planet is traced directly to creative actions of God, and that those creative actions were only a few thousand years ago, passions can flare.

Interestingly, often an excluded voice in discussion of origins are those religious persons who agree with some points from both groups. This third group agrees that there is a great deal of commonality between species and that mutation over time is able to account for much of what we observe in the world today. They also agree that life itself is best explained by creative actions of God. In fact, the existence of the universe is best explained as the result of God's creative action.

Unfortunately, passions from this discussion remain heated, and not only divide the religious from the nonreligious, but also the religious from one another. One point where all of the religious groups can come to an agreement, especially Christians, should be on the idea that God created humans. We may disagree about the way God created humans, but we should agree that, however God did it, he is the one responsible for humanity.

Those who reject the concept that God created the human race will obviously disagree with this position, but this work is not directed toward the nonreligious. The assumption of this chapter is that God is responsible for humanity, and this work does not take a position on the manner in which God created. Arguments about how God created are interesting, but not relevant to the purpose of this work.

GOD WAS FREE TO CREATE

God created humans because he wanted to. Christians teach that God did not have to create anything at all, the act of creation was a "free" action. God did not become greater because he created the universe. God was just as glorious without creation. The freedom God had in choosing to create or not is an important aspect of who God is and why he created anything at all.

Some religions do not see that God was free to create or not to create. Some religious systems require that God had to create the universe so that he could relate to something. For God to show love, for example, he would need to have something different than himself to be the object of that love. A monotheism where God is a radical unity would require God to create something in order for him to love it. In that kind of understanding of God (like we find in Islam), God cannot love without the creation for him to love. Creation is needed, or necessary, for God. If that is the case, then God would not create out of freedom, but God would be compelled to create so that he could have an object to love.

Christians do not have this issue because of our understanding of God as Trinity. Without creation, the Father, Son, and Spirit were in perfect harmony. Each member of the Trinity could love the other members. The Triune God of Christianity did not need to create anything in order to express love. Creation is a free action. Nothing made or compelled God to create this universe. God was not lacking an object of affection that resulted in him creating humanity. God was free to create or not create.

God Did Not Need to Create

Why is this an issue? Why do we care if God had to create or if God's creative action was free? What difference does that make? Some people may ask those questions when we begin to examine the issue of God's freedom to create or not. On one hand, it seems like a legitimate question. Since God has actually created, why would we worry about whether or not he had to create? From a very practical side, it may not matter whether God had to create the universe or whether it was a free action. God did create the universe and we simply have to move on.

Understanding that God's act of creation was a free action helps us to have more confidence in his purposes. Whether God's creative action was free or necessary may not make a lot of difference in the decisions we make on a day-to-day basis, it does clarify our understanding of God's purposes.

Christianity holds that God was able to create any possible universe he wanted. In fact, when we examine how the universe could have been, simply by altering physical forces and/or quantities of matter by the smallest amount, the universe would have been quite different. A small change in the value of certain forces or the quantity of matter could lead to universes where stars and planets never formed. Without stars and planets, life as we know it would not be possible.

Christian theology affirms that God could have created a universe without life. God could have created a universe with nothing in it but space and time if he wanted. God could have created a universe that consisted of a single star to shine for his glory. God could have created any possible universe or no universe, because he is free.

If God was not free to create, then there might be certain aspects of the creation that God was also not free in creating. For example, what if God had to triumph over an evil adversary? If God required an evil adversary to overcome in the same way that a God who needed an object to love would be forced to create an object, then would God have to create an evil adversary? It seems that the answer would be yes. But if that were the case, what would that mean for God's creation?

It might mean that might there would also be constraints on what God would have to create. For example, if God had to create an evil adversary, he would be limited in the types of universes he could create, since all of the available universes would have to contain the adversary. God could not create the universe with nothing but space and time or the universe with a single star, because he would have to include the adversary.

If the adversary had to have certain necessary characteristics, then even more restrictions would be placed on the type of universe available. If the adversary had to be physical, then any universe God would create would have to have the appropriate matter for the adversary's physical nature. If the adversary were much like a human, then the universe would have to be able to support humanlike life.

As we suggest possible restrictions on the types of universes God could have created, God's freedom becomes limited. A God that cannot freely create might have had to create the universe as it is. If God had to create the universe the way it is, how do we know that God's ultimate purposes will be accomplished? If God was not free to create, he might not have had any choice in the creation of humanity. Instead of humans being a special creation of God, humans may be a necessary component of a universe God did not want to create. We might not be special at all. In fact, we might just be cogs in a gear of a universe that an unfree God was forced to create.

God Chose to Create for His Own Purposes

Christianity does not accept the idea that God was forced to create anything. One of the reasons Christians see creation as a free act is because of the problems with the concept of God being forced to create. Another reason is because Scripture tells us that God did create humans with a special purpose and the Bible tells us that God is free to do as he wills (Dan 4:35). As the Psalmist writes, "Our God is in heaven; he does whatever pleases him" (Ps 115:3).

Christians reject the idea that God was forced to create at all. Because God was free in his creation, he created for his own purposes and his own ends. We can have confidence that God's purposes will be accomplished because nothing could compel him to create anything other than what he desired to create. If there was something about the created order God did not want, he could have changed it or not created at all. God's freedom in creation is important for Christians because we can believe what God has told us about his purposes and intentions for us and the rest of the created order.

Humans are a special part of creation

God was free to create, and he created. The creation is massive and awe-inspiring. The sheer expanse of the universe is beyond our ability to grasp. With our limited frame of reference, it is difficult to comprehend just how small and seemingly insignificant we are. Even within our own galaxy or within our own solar system, our planet is very small. When we consider that each one of us is similarly insignificant in relationship to the size of our planet, the point is driven home all the more. On a cosmic level, humanity and our planet are a tiny insignificant speck.

God, however, considers humanity to be very special. We are dear to the Creator of the universe. Our value to God is not because we are particularly valuable to the cosmos. Without us, the universe would keep on doing what it does with little noticeable effect. In fact, many humans are born, live, and die every day, and the universe is indifferent to us. While the universe may not care (or even have the capacity to care), God told us that he does care. God cares a lot.

Humans Image God

One of the reasons God cares about humanity is that we are made in his image. No other creature is said to be made in God's image. God's servants who dwell in his presence are not said to be made in his image. Angels may be more powerful than humans, but they are not image bearers of the divine. Angels may have special access and responsibilities before God, but they are not said to be made in his likeness. Likewise, demons may be more powerful, intelligent, and crafty than humans, but only humanity is said to be made in God's image.

Are humans unique? Could other beings be made in God's image? As far as we know, we are unique. But we should remember that our universe is vast, our God is free, and our God is not only limited to this universe.

Within the vastness of the universe, God could have other creatures that are also made in his image. If they were to exist, they may or may not resemble humanity. God is free to do as he pleases and if he wanted to make other creatures in his image he certainly could. Whether he made other creatures in his image in our universe, we don't know.

God is also beyond our universe. He could have created other universes that are separate from ours. If God did create other universes, he might have created other creatures that bear his image in those other universes. But none of this should trouble us. Being made in God's image is special in its own right.

If God did create only humanity in his image or there are other creatures who also image God, the important part to remember is that humans are made in the image of God. The possibility of other image-bearing creatures notwithstanding, humans bear God's image. Bearing God's image is enough to make us special.

Humans Relate to God Differently than the Rest of the Creation

As image bearers, humans relate to God differently than the rest of the creation. Since we know of no other creatures who bear God's image, we assume that humanity alone relates to God as image-bearing creatures. The rest of the creation relates to God as creatures.

All of creation, including humanity, relates to God as creature to Creator. God has complete authority over all aspects of his creation. God can choose to do what he will with any part of his creation. Sun, moon, stars, animals, galaxies—whatever exists does so at God's good pleasure. The created order has no right to existence. As part of that created order, humans have no right to their own existence. We only exist at the pleasure of God.

Unlike the rest of creation, we have a connection to God beyond the fact he created us. He created us a certain way, in his image, and because of that we identify both with the created order and with the Creator. Christians have struggled throughout the centuries attempting to figure out what exactly is the image of God in humanity, but the fact that we possess it is without dispute.

Our connection with God is unique when compared with the non-image-bearing creatures. That means that our connection to God is even different from the way the angelic hosts of heaven relate to God. Our special connection to God might be what causes us to long for him. Being made in God's image may provide the urge within humanity to seek transcendence.

Humans Relate to Creation Differently

Being made in God's image means that we have a connection to God that is different than the rest of creation. It also means that we relate to other creatures differently than they relate to one another. As image bearers, we are not the same as other creatures. We may be able to relate to them on certain levels, such as the fact that we need food and rest. But we are not completely like they are. We know this. Many western people have pets for companionship. But no matter how hard we may try to erase our difference, we have differences that will remain.

We can find great solace and comfort in creation, but there are certain relationships we are lacking when we find ourselves relating only to the non-image-bearing parts of the creation. The longing we have to relate to something more than the created order drives us to find relationships with both God and other humans. Perhaps the divine image within us will not allow us to find our ultimate contentment in that which is created. Maybe the divine image is the place where our longing for God resides. As Augustine wrote, "You have made us for yourself and our hearts are restless until they find their rest in you" (*Conf.* 1.1.1)

Humans Relate to other Humans Uniquely

Finally, humans relate to other humans in a unique way. We are the only creatures bearing God's image. We struggle to relate to non-image-bearing creatures and to God himself. Only other humans have the same types of struggles. We are social creatures and need human relationships also. God recognized this and created woman to be with man. "The Lord God said, 'It is not good for the man to be alone. I will make a helper suitable for him'" (Gen 2:18).

There is a goodness about humans relating to other humans. Christians will often cite Paul and Jesus telling Christians to be in the world but not of the world. Perhaps we are both of the world and not of the world. We belong to the created realm, but due to bearing the image of God, we also belong to the realm beyond the creation. That type of struggle is one that only humans can experience. We relate to one another as creatures struggling with both belonging and not belonging to the place where we are.

GOD HAS A PURPOSE FOR HUMANITY

God created freely and with his own purposes in mind. He also made humans special within his creation. Humans were created to fulfill a purpose, or rather, to fulfill purposes that God has in mind. God's creation itself is marked by his intention. Some people have said that the universe has God's fingerprints all over it. God reveals himself in the created order and we should expect that the creation would be patterned after God's characteristics.

> I make known the end from the beginning, from ancient times, what is still to come. I say, "My purpose will stand, and I will do all that I please." (Isa 46:10)

God is Ordered and Rational

> Oh, the depth of the riches of the wisdom and knowledge of God! How unsearchable his judgments, and his paths beyond tracing out! (Rom 11:23)

As we look at the created order, we notice patterns. We observe events and suppose their causes. With the advent of the scientific method, we make observations and test hypotheses in an attempt to better understand the processes that make up the physical universe. We have had some good success in figuring out how this universe works. One of the reasons we expect the universe to operate with a degree of rationality and order is because God is rational and ordered.

The doctrine of creation from nothing (*creatio ex nihilo*) was one of the important concepts in beginning to look at the world as an ordered and rational system. Prior to an understanding that the world is distinct from God, many peoples viewed the world as a place inhabited by spirits. The earth itself was sometimes understood to be the carcass of a god.

In the Mesopotamian creation story known as the *Enuma Elish*, the world came into existence because a god, Marduk, killed a goddess, Tiamat. After slaying her, he ripped her body in two. One half of Tiamat became the heavens, and the other half of Tiamat became the earth. This story continues by describing humanity's origin. Marduk kills another god, Kingu, who was Tiamat's ally. Kingu's blood is used to create humans, and humanity's purpose is to serve the gods.

Given the Mesopotamian view of the world, everyone is walking around on the corpse of a dead goddess. Strange things might happen if someone were to dissect a goddess. People may have feared releasing magic if they began to poke and prod around to learn more about the way the world works. Whether people believed that the Earth was perched on the back of a giant turtle, held up by Atlas, or was the corpse of Tiamat, it was not until the concept that God created a world distinct from himself that the world became demystified. Exploration and discovery, within a created, ordered, and rational world become not only paths to gain knowledge, but a way to glorify God.

Early modern scientists often felt like their pursuit of knowledge was a way to bring further glory to God in addition to any benefit it may have for humanity. Nicolaus Copernicus, a mathematician and astronomer of the Renaissance, developed the heliocentric model of the universe and was a Christian. Galileo and Kepler were also Christians. Isaac Newton, whose laws dominated physics for three centuries, wrote religious tracts. Robert Boyle, best known for his work with gas pressure and volume, funded missionaries and supported translating the Bible into the common language of a people.

The theological conception that God created the universe, and that it is not part of God, liberated humanity's creative power and investigative imagination. Indeed, the idea that the Book of Nature witnesses to God just like the Bible was a factor in men pursuing a deeper understanding of the world.

> I was merely thinking God's thoughts after him. Since we astronomers are priests of the highest God in regard to the book of nature, it benefits us to be thoughtful, not of the glory of our minds, but rather, above all else, of the glory of God. —Johann Kepler[1]

God's Creation Fulfilled His Purpose

God has a goal for creation. Certain parts of God's plan have been revealed, but much is beyond humanity's grasp. One of God's purposes for the creation was to demonstrate his own glory.

> The heavens declare the glory of God; the skies proclaim the work of his hands. Day after day they pour forth speech; night after night they reveal knowledge. They have no speech, they use no words; no sound is heard from them. Yet their voice goes out into all the earth, their words to the ends of the world (Ps 19:1–4).

God is most glorious and powerful. The magnitude of the created order testifies to his power. As we learn more about the universe, we find that our conception of God only grows. When the psalmist wrote of God's glory, he

1. New World Encyclopedia, "Johannes Kepler," para. 52.

had a big view of God. Imagery in the Bible portrays God as so large that the dust raised from his footsteps are like the clouds. That is a massive image, a kind of powerful that kings can rage against, but could never overcome.

As we began to understand that our planet was one of several that orbited our sun, our conception of God expanded to account for the twirling of planets. The idea that God's footsteps caused dust like the clouds of the sky was now inadequate. The moon itself would be out of his reach, if God was powerful like a massive giant. To order the planets and stars, God would have to be much more powerful than anything centered around our Earth.

As we have come to understand the vast nature of the universe and the massive amount of material, stars, planets, galaxies, and distance beyond our ability to grasp, God must be viewed as proportionally more powerful than we might have imagined. The more we learn about the created order, the more we realize that God is so much greater than we could have imagined previously. When we think of the great achievements of humanity and the power we have amassed, we have still come no closer to achieving God's level of power. God is still infinitely beyond us, and the more we know the more we realize what we have left to learn.

The creation testifies to God's greatness and the testimony becomes greater as we venture to learn more. Creation also allows God's creatures to express their adoration for their Creator. Stars can shine for God's glory or explode in praise. Comets can streak throughout the cosmos as a declaration of the greatness of God. Angels bow down and worship. We may only be able to faintly hear the echoes of worship given to the Creator from the distant corners of his creation. But it testifies, groans, sings, and shouts praise and worship to God for all who will listen.

God's Purpose in Creation Includes Humanity

God is glorified and worshiped by his creation. The parts of the creation that do not bear his image still declare his glory. Humans, who are image bearers, also have a purpose in God's creation. The purpose for humanity includes praising and worshiping God, just like the non-image-bearing creation, but God has more in mind for us. We are also designed to find satisfaction in God.

We share a type of transcendence over the physical world: we can have intentions, goals, and desires. We can choose to direct what little transcendence we have to submission or opposition to God.

God's plan includes humanity serving him as representatives in the creation. Dominion will be discussed later in this chapter, but in addition to praising and worshiping God, we are also representatives of God in his creation. God did not need a gardener, but it pleased him to create Adam. Adam shared much with the creation he was to oversee, but he also shared something with the God who placed him there to oversee it.

Humanity was not an afterthought. God planed for humanity to be a bridge between the created and the divine. Humans are creatures, totally dependent on God for all that we are. We are material, finite, flawed, and weak. We have all the limitations of any creature. However, we also have a heritage that is beyond the creation. We are beings made of flesh and blood, but we bear the image of the Creator. There is more to humanity than matter—we beam with God's representation. Humanity is valuable because of God's plan for us and of our relationship to God.

GOD REVEALED HIS PURPOSE

God has not left his creation without guidance. He wrote his purposes and intentions for his people in the heavens and on our hearts. He fashioned creation to cry out his glory. God has revealed himself through what he has created and to his creation. The two common theological terms are General Revelation and Special Revelation.

> General Revelation: God's self-disclosure through nature, history, and human faculties.
>
> Special Revelation: God's personal self-disclosure through acts in history, divine speech, and the incarnation.

Through General Revelation

General Revelation can be thought of as revelation through the creation. It is impersonal. The creation is the means by which the revelation is communicated. Waiting to be observed, the creation goes about its business of revealing God whether or not anyone other than God is observing. The heavens are declaring and the skies are proclaiming (Psalm 19).

The creation is not just the medium through which revelation is transmitted; is also the content of the transmission. The heavens are declaring God's glory, and they are the declaration. The skies are proclaiming God's glory, and they are the proclamation. The creation comes from God, declares his glory, and is itself the declaration of God's glory. General Revelation is mediated through the creation, and is by nature a step further removed than Special Revelation.

Through Special Revelation

Special Revelation is personal. A better way to put this is that Special Revelation is revealed to persons. While entire galaxies on the other side of the universe may declare God's glory as loudly as our own galaxy does, we have not observed them. We may never observe them. In areas of the universe, God may receive glory from his creation that no one except him will ever witness. Not so with Special Revelation. Special Revelation is revealed to persons.

The Old Testament accounts of God's acting in history are some of our most vivid accounts of God revealing himself to people. By revealing himself through the burning bush, giving the law, and other encounters, God made himself known to Moses. Jacob wrestled with God. God roused young Samuel from his bed to tell him of the impending fall of Eli. Over and over we see God revealing himself in personal ways to people.

Special Revelation also took place by acts of history. Directing the Israelites to Egypt with the famine, saving them through Joseph's works, and later liberating them from Egypt are all actions of God by which he revealed himself to his people. While the Egyptian exodus is a magnificent series of actions, from the plagues to the parting of the Red Sea, they are not the only historical events by which God revealed himself. The conquest of Canaan and other military victories against Israel's enemies are also examples of such events.

Covenants as Revelation

The covenants with God are types of special revelation. This section will examine how God revealed himself in two covenants with his people.

God made several covenants with humans. Generally, a covenant is an agreement, similar to what we know as contracts. Covenants could be between people who were essentially equals, or they could be between people who had drastically different statuses. In the case of God's covenants with humans, it is clear that God is immeasurably superior to humans, and the covenants that God makes contain elements of commands and guarantees from God. The specifics of the covenant reveal things about God and his purposes. The covenant was special revelation between the individuals receiving them and God, and the accounts of these covenants as recorded in Scripture are also revelation.

In Genesis, God establishes a covenant with Noah. God tells Noah, "I establish my covenant with you: Never again will all life be destroyed by the waters of a flood; never again will there be a flood to destroy the earth" (Gen 9:11). This covenant is one in which God assures humans and the other living creatures that he will not put them through the judgment of a flood again. It may also include a promise of regular seasons. Regardless, the covenant is a guarantee from God. Noah is also blessed by God and given dominion over the animals, and the animals are caused to fear humans.

The Noachian Covenant reveals that God is compassionate and merciful. The flood was a terrible judgment and threw the natural systems out of their normal courses. Entire ecosystems were obliterated, and regularity of the seasons were suspended. The wickedness of mankind deserved the destruction that God wrought, but God will not bring that kind of judgment on the world again. The compassion could be for the sake of the other living creatures, or it could be for the destruction of humanity, or some combination of both. The point is that God extends grace to the creation, particularly to the Earth. Although utter destruction is due, God will not utterly destroy the Earth again.

Giving Noah the animals for food is merciful to Noah since food would be scarce until the vegetation could regrow following the deluge. Some of the animals God brought through the flood would serve as food for Noah. God was also merciful to the animals making them fear humans, so that they could survive and reproduce.

Noah is also commanded to reproduce. God intended humanity to increase in number and to fill the Earth. God demonstrated his longsuffering in this command. Even though humans were inclined to do evil (Gen 8:24), Noah is commanded to be fruitful and multiply. God knows that Noah's descendants will do much evil, but he wants them to exist in spite of this fact.

Moses was also a recipient of a covenant with God. The Sinaitic Covenant is much more elaborate than the covenant with Noah, as it includes the law. This covenant provides many specific behaviors for God's people and regulates how they relate to God, one another, and people outside of the covenant. It includes the Decalogue, or the Ten Commandments, and the Israelites agreed to be bound by it.

This covenant also reveals aspects of God's character. God loves and provides for humanity. The covenant's purpose was to keep the people from sinning (Exod 20:21). Knowing humanity's propensity to sin, God provided a way for people to avoid sin. The law also shows that God is just. When people are wronged, or have a loss, some aspects of the law allow for proper recovery. In a perfect world, people would naturally compensate others for wrongs, and God provides specific details because humans often fail to do right.

Called People as Revelation

When God calls people to serve him, he reveals himself in a unique way. This section will examine God's call of three individuals (Samuel, Jonah, and Paul) as recorded in Scripture, specifically how God is revealed in those encounters.

God revealed himself to a boy serving under the leadership of the priest Eli, who had been warned that his family would be judged for the actions of his sons and his failure to stop the abuses. Hophni and Phinehas treated the offerings given to the Lord with contempt. They chose to ignore what God had provided and take for themselves what they wanted, and Eli did not stop them.

Samuel was being prepared by God while these abuses were happening. One evening, God spoke to Samuel and confirmed that the pronounced judgments were going to take place. God used Samuel as a prophet for many years to lead his people, including when Israel chose to have a king.

God's love for his people and his concern that they worship him properly is demonstrated in the calling of Samuel. Hophni and Phinehas are abusing God's people and their position, and Eli is either unable or unwilling to stop his sons. God refuses to allow this travesty to stand and intervenes himself. Samuel is called to guide God's people back to proper worship and toward justice. God revealed himself through Samuel's life and ministry, as well as through his words.

In a way similar to Samuel, God also revealed himself through Jonah, giving him a task to deliver a prophecy to Nineveh. The Assyrian residents were despised by God's people, as they worshiped false gods and were positively brutal. Jonah attempts to flee his calling and boards a ship to head away from where God called him. Instead, God uses a storm and a sea creature to reveal himself to Jonah and the sailors. Eventually Jonah delivers God's message in Nineveh and the people of the city repent. However, Jonah is angry that the people repent and that God does not destroy them. God then grows and destroys a plant in a day to teach Jonah about his care for the people of Nineveh.

God's love for people outside of his chosen people is demonstrated in Jonah's calling to Nineveh, but Jonah does not like or approve of what God is doing in offering mercy to people Jonah despised. However, God does not allow the sinfulness of Jonah to prevent his will from coming about, revealing his nature to Ninevah with words in response to Jonah's disobedience.

Finally, God revealed himself to someone who was persecuting his people. Paul (then known as Saul) was seeking to destroy the fledgling church. God revealed himself on the road to Damascus in a spectacular way. Saul was blind for three days before God sent Ananias to heal him. Saul, who was later known as Paul, was used by God to spread the gospel to the gentiles, and he was also used to write a large portion of Scripture.

God's love for those who are attacking his people is demonstrated in the conversion and calling of Paul—not only does God remove a threat to his church, but he also gains a powerful figure to lead his people. God revealed himself to Paul in a vision and in blindness, through his life and ministry, and through Paul's writings to the churches.

Scripture as Revelation

God revealed himself to his people through the written word. We call this our Scriptures or the Bible. Although what is contained in Scripture is the result of God working through people and in accordance with his covenants, as mentioned above, Scripture is itself revelation of God. This section will examine how God reveals himself through his written word.

> By direct command, a sense of urgency, or simply a personal desire or compulsion, God's spirit moved spiritual persons within

the faith community to write or compile from dictation, experience, tradition, or wisdom those documents which reflect what God desired to have recorded in order that his purposes might be served.[2]

God revealed himself in a unique way to the writers of Scripture. The Bible itself records different ways God revealed himself to people. Sometimes God had people make written records of his revelation that we call Scripture.

We do not have any way of knowing everything that God revealed to the Scripture writers, but we know that they did not record everything God revealed to them. It is safe to say that there was more revealed than was recorded, but we can also say that God led people to record what he intended for them to record.

The term we use for the idea that Scriptures come from God is inspiration. Inspiration is God directing the composition of Scripture so that his revelation is properly recorded. The involvement of the Holy Spirit in inspiration allows us to have more than simply records of revelation; it allows for those records of revelation to themselves be revelation of God. Because of the work of the Holy Spirit in producing Scripture, Scripture is revelation.

Through Jesus Christ

The most significant of God's revelation is Jesus Christ himself. This section will examine how God revealed himself as Jesus Christ.

> The Word became flesh and made his dwelling among us. We have seen his glory, the glory of the one and only Son, who came from the Father, full of grace and truth. (John 1:14)

Jesus Christ is the best revelation of God. When God took on human flesh, the most amazing miracle of all time took place. God, who is transcendent, took on a material body. The Creator of the universe, not bound by things outside of himself, became limited as all humans are limited.

Those who saw Jesus saw God in the flesh. The complete revelation of God walked the earth as the man Jesus Christ. Any shortcomings in revelation that took place prior to Jesus were made complete in his revelation of God. Jesus clarified teachings that the Jewish people practiced. Jesus spoke with authority about certain issues of religious debate. He gave his followers teachings that reflected God's heart and intent. He showed his followers

---

2. Grenz, *Community of God*, 382.

how to be "true Israel." Jesus showed the way to have a relationship with God that was more intimate than before. Through Jesus' teachings, people could become adopted into God's family.

God revealed himself directly to select people before Jesus, and those select prophets in turn communicated God to others. Jesus was unique in that God's revelation as Jesus was direct to more people. Although many more people received direct revelation from God during Jesus' ministry, not everyone who received that revelation accepted it. In fact, many rejected Jesus. The Gospel accounts attest to the manifold rejection of Jesus by his own people. Like many prophets before him, Jesus was killed for his revelation of God, the most complete revelation of God that has taken place. However, more importantly, we must remember that Jesus also redeemed humanity.

Through the church

From the surprised followers of Jesus who huddled together after the resurrection appearances to the modern day, God has revealed himself through his church. The mere existence of God's church is a revelation of his love and care for humanity. God reveals himself through the life and functions of the church and her family. This section will examine how God has revealed himself in the church.

The Apostolic church

God revealed himself directly to the apostles and others who encountered Jesus while he was on earth. In turn, they taught the church what Jesus had taught to them. They also began to find other teachings about God in the Old Testament writings that made more sense to them after they understood Jesus' mission and what he had accomplished.

The church of the apostles, then, revealed God in a way similar to the way the prophets did. They were the second level, revealing Jesus to others based on how Jesus had revealed himself to them. The direct revelation did not stop with the ascension of Jesus, however; they also received revelation of God from the Holy Spirit. Through the indwelling of the Holy Spirit, the apostles were able to reveal God to the church from four sources. The four sources were as follows: 1) direct interaction with Jesus, 2) indirect interaction with God through reading of the Old Testament, 3) direct interaction with the indwelling Holy Spirit, and 4) indirect interaction with God through non-Scriptural traditions.[3]

The apostles had access to Jesus in a way that modern Christians do not. They were vital for the early church because of the connection they had to Jesus. Thankfully, because of the apostles, we have the Gospels as records of their encounters with Jesus. The New Testament provides us with valuable insights from the apostolic church that would be missing if we did not have it.

The Church After the Apostles

After the apostles died, the church continued. The church continues to reveal God by its existence and by the teachings that have come from her. After the time of the apostles, church leadership no longer could claim the direct contact with Jesus. The only contact with Jesus that people could claim was indirect through relationships with the apostles (a claim now held by the Catholic and Orthodox churches) and through the writings of the New Testament.

Fortunately, the indirect connections to Jesus are sufficient for understanding Jesus' revelation of God. Church leaders since the apostles have only been able to claim three sources of revelation from God. The three sources are 1) indirect interaction with God through the reading of the Bible and/or the unpublished teachings of the apostles (the Catholic view); 2) direct interaction with the indwelling of the Holy Spirit; and 3) indirect interaction with God through non-Scriptural traditions.

The church still has access to information about God that is special. Although some sources of revelation are available outside of the church, the indwelling of the Holy Spirit is unique to believing Christians, which, by definition, make up the universal church.

---

3. By non-Scriptural traditions, I mean writings or oral traditions by thinkers or theologians that contain information about God but are not themselves Scripture. Commentary on biblical books are examples, as are theological writings. This book is an example of a non-Scriptural work that contains revealed information about God.

Created for Relationship

GOD REDEEMED HIS PEOPLE TO FULFILL HIS PURPOSE

At the heart of God's purpose for his creation is to bring it (and particularly humans) into a relationship with himself. In order to bring humans into a loving and trusting relationship, God planned to overcome some of our self-imposed obstacles to being in relationship with him. God knew he would need to overcome both our limitations as creatures and our rebellion against him. God's plan included the redemption of his people throughout history.

Pre-Fall

Before humanity fell into sin, our ultimate forebears had a relationship with God in the bliss of the garden of Eden. God walked with Adam, and the relationship was unmarred by rebellion and deceit. Adam and Eve had the task of tending to the garden, whatever that entailed. We don't have clear descriptions of their tasks in the text, but they had things to be about. While they did their tasks, God would commune with them.

Unsurprisingly, not much of Genesis passes before our ancestors breach God's commands and the world ends up much more difficult and dangerous. The time before the fall is brief (in terms of attention given in Scripture) and serves as the stage from which the drama of the relationship of creature to Creator unfolds.

Pre-Flood

The world after the fall of humanity becomes evil quickly. Of the first four humans we meet in the biblical narrative, one of them, Cain, kills another, his brother Abel, early in the Genesis account. From the first recorded murder, things continue to spiral into more evil and depravity. Generally, humans just seem to be disinterested in knowing God.

In fact, the world quickly becomes so overrun with evil that God decides to destroy the wickedness of the people.

> The Lord saw how great the wickedness of the human race had become on the earth, and that every inclination of the thoughts of the human heart was only evil all the time. The Lord regretted that he had made human beings on the earth, and his heart was deeply troubled. So the Lord said, "I will wipe from the face of the earth

> the human race I have created—and with them the animals, the birds and the creatures that move along the ground—for I regret that I have made them." But Noah found favor in the eyes of the Lord. (Gen 6:5–8)

God did not destroy all that he created. Noah was one whom God favored. He would be preserved, along with his family, from the judgment that was coming on the wicked world.

The pre-flood era shows us how quickly humanity can fall into great sin and evil. In Genesis 6, we are told that humanity has gotten so bad that God regretted making them, and back in Genesis 1, the creation was declared to be good. The fall itself does not occur until chapter 3, so in two chapters the world becomes so evil that God decided to bring severe judgment.

Humanity, left to its own desires, will seek evil at a breathtaking pace. God would have to intervene in extraordinary ways to accomplish his purposes with humans. After addressing the evil in the world during Noah's day, God sets events in motion that will lead to the redemption of his people.

Abrahamic Covenant

God enters into a special relationship with Abram. He calls him from his home and takes him to a new place. He promises him that he will have many descendants, but delays the fulfillment of that promise until late in life. Then, after the child of promise is born, God asks him to sacrifice his treasured child. God demonstrates a commitment to Abraham that is unique and special.

With Abraham, God promised to bless him. The promised blessing will extend beyond Abraham to the entire world. The blessing will take a long time to arrive. Abraham's story shows a man who is impatient to receive his blessing, and who even tries to force God's hand by having a child with Hagar. God did not allow Abraham's impatience or lack of trust to deter his plans. God fulfilled his promise and Sarah gave birth to Isaac. Abraham's lack of patience and trust in God resulted in the birth of Ishmael. Later, Abraham was able to demonstrate his personal growth and how he was able to trust God. When God commanded him to sacrifice Isaac, he was obedient and trusted God.

Abraham grew in his relationship with God. Early in life he did not have sufficient patience or trust to be faithful to God. Later, after many years of waiting, watching, and learning to trust, he was able to trust God with the life of his own son. Abraham's story demonstrates that humans can have a trusting relationship with God, even though we will be impatient and we will be slow to trust God as we should.

Mosiaic Covenant

Abraham's story takes many more turns and plot twists before we are introduced to Moses. Some of Abraham's descendants are suffering in Egypt, and God hears their cry. God raises Moses to lead his people out of Egypt and back to the land promised to them. The Exodus story and the wilderness wanderings teach us much about God and our problems following where God leads.

Eventually, God provides the law to Moses so that his people will be able to live in relationship to God properly. A formalized system of worshiping God and living in community as his people will serve as a guide for how humans can properly relate to God and one another. Just getting to the point where the statutes are available is difficult enough. God's people are shown to be as impatient as Abraham was. They are also shown to lack trust in God, just like Abraham did. The refusal to trust God leads to the wilderness wandering period and a delay in receiving the promised land.

When God's people have the law, they have explicit instructions on how they should live, worship God, and order their lives. Following the law will demonstrate trust in God. The nation of people are brought into a closer relationship with God by trusting God and implementing his law. Finally, God brings his people into the promised land. The people of God now have a home, as well as the means to properly relate to God and one another.

In the Promised Land

Moses never gets to live in the promised land, but God's people do. They enjoy the blessings of the land and of the law. Humans have difficulty remaining faithful, however, and quickly begin to ignore the law. They enjoy living in the blessings, but don't like keeping up their obligations.

God's people fail over and over again to remain faithful to God and his law. In order to show them that they need him, God allows trouble to come upon them. He then delivers his people from that trouble to show his own faithfulness. The people return to God in gratitude, but over time they fall away again. Evidently, humans seem to have a problem remaining faithful to God when living in a blessing. Trials and difficulty tend to make people realize the need for God, but the realization is itself short-lived.

God remains faithful when his people are not. He honors his covenant, when his people ignore it. God's people struggle to stay in relationship with him. Blessings from God seem to mask the need for him, and his people wander. When the blessings are removed and difficulty comes, the need for God comes to the surface and his people return to him. Unfortunately, the return to fellowship is only temporary.

Life in the promised land showed that God's people would only be in a loving and trusting relationship with God on an intermittent basis. God's intervention is necessary to correct the wandering that characterized his people.

In Exile and Back Again

Time showed that living in the promised land failed to produce a people who would remain in faithful relationship with God. God had allowed threats and dangers to come to his people and then saved them to show his faithfulness. If living in the promise was not enough for his people to be faithful, he would allow them to be expelled from the promised land. Exile comes to God's people.

In exile, the people once again realized that they needed God. The exile period shows how God is faithful to his people, even when they are not in the promised land. The people lived in a foreign land with an expectation that they would return home and one day live again in God's promise. Eventually, God brought his people back to his promise and showed himself faithful. However, initial repentance and gratitude for God's love and faithfulness is soon forgotten. Exile shows that losing the blessing of the promise, even for generations, will not produce a people who remain in a loving and trusting relationship with God. God's people will wander away from his laws. They will come back to them, but only with suffering and hardship.

The exile of God's people and the subsequent return to the promised land demonstrates God's faithfulness and the persistent inability of God's people to remain faithful. God does not desire an intermittent relationship with his people. God desires an enduring, intimate relationship with his people. The law, which allows God's people to demonstrate their love and trust in him, ends up being a barrier to relationship. It is a barrier, not because it is flawed, but because humans are fickle.

In Christ

The phrase "If you want something done right, do it yourself," attributed to French playwright Charles-Guillaume Ètienne, could be used to describe the incarnation of Jesus Christ. Humans proved unable to live in a loving and trusting relationship with God. Human sin and lack of trust provided a relationship with God that was intermittent at best and often rebellious. God's purposes included humans, and their inability to live up to what he had planned would not deter him. Jesus came to live a perfect life and fulfill the law in our place.

Jesus accomplished what humans were unable to do by faithfully living in a loving and trusting relationship with God. He remained faithful to the Father throughout his life and at the cost of it. His faithfulness overcame our unfaithfulness. His sinlessness overcame our sinfulness. His trust overcame our lack of trust. His sacrifice overcame our guilt. Jesus' life, death, and resurrection provided a way for humanity to relate to God in a loving and trusting relationship that was not based on our ability to remain faithful.

Where the law had provided a way for certain humans to live in a loving and trusting relationship with God, Jesus provided the loving and trusting relationship for humans. While humans were unable to faithfully keep the law, Jesus did. His faithfulness and suffering allowed for reconciliation between God and humanity. He paid the penalty for our unfaithfulness and allowed us to gain the reward of his faithfulness. In this way, humanity has been reconciled to God solely on the merit of Jesus Christ.

God and humans are able to be in a loving and trusting relationship that will endure because of Jesus. Jesus' relationship with God is the basis for our relationship with God. By having a relationship with Jesus, we partake in the relationship between Jesus and the Father. Human relationship with God, apart from Christ, will be intermittent at best. Jesus' relationship to the Father is perfect and complete. God's relationship to humanity, mediated through Jesus, is permanent. In Jesus, God's purpose of having a loving and trusting relationship with humanity is accomplished. Humanity is redeemed through Christ.

In the Church

After Jesus reconciled humanity to God, the story did not end. Jesus lived and died in one small part of the world. God's people were always supposed to glorify God so that other peoples and nations would be drawn to him. God did not intend for only a small portion of the human population to be in relationship with him. God's people were to represent God to the world and to be a conduit for God to bless all of the peoples of the earth.

God's people in relationship with God because of Jesus, or the church, began to share the gospel of Jesus Christ. The church spread from the promised land through the Roman Empire and beyond. In the church, relationship with God is available to people through the world. In the church, God will complete his purpose of bringing humans into a loving and trusting relationship with himself. The culmination of this purpose will include peoples from all over the Earth.

God has overcome many obstacles to allow humans to be in a loving and trusting relationship with him. God overcame our sin and rebellion. God overcame our fickle nature that kept us from being faithful to him. God reconciled the world to himself in Christ Jesus and made a way for us to have a permanent relationship with him. God is now moving through the church to complete his purpose of having a loving and trusting relationship with humanity.

GOD DETERMINES WHAT IT MEANS TO BE HUMAN

> What is mankind that you are mindful of them, human beings that you care for them? You have made them a little lower than the angels and crowned them with glory and honor. (Ps 8: 4–5)

Humans were created by God for his own purposes. Humans owe no one other than God for our existence. Not only did God create humanity, God determined all of the human characteristics. From our physical nature, our being made of skin and bones, to our intellect and emotional capacities, God is the one who designed and produced human beings.

God, being the Creator of everything that is created, chose what characteristics each creature would possess. Within God's intentions lie the framework or form of each individual and each class of creature. In other words, whatever characteristics God designed for humans are the set of characteristics that define humanity. In addition to defining the ontological aspect of creation, God also defined value and responsibilities for his creation as well.

God's Intention is the Basis for Value

If God is the Creator of all, then the only objective value in the creation is based on God's assessment. Creatures may value something other than what God does. The fact that a creature values something differently than God does not diminish or increase the objective value given by God.

God is the Ground of Existence

Humanity would not exist if God had not created it. The cause for humans coming into existence is God's creative action. The reason that humanity persists in existence is because of God's preservation of his creation. Without God acting to create and to preserve, nothing (including humans) would exist.

Human existence, along with all other created beings, is fixed and grounded in God's existence. If we suppose that God were not to exist, we would have to suppose another ground for the existence of the universe in general and humanity in particular.

Value Comes from God's Creative Acts and Intentions

God's act of creation and the creatures resulting from that act are good. Whatever God intends for the creatures he created to do is the thing that those creatures should do. Humans, for example, were created and given a task of tending to the garden. Tending to the garden, as God instructed, would be an example of proper behavior. Likewise, neglecting it would be an example of improper behavior.

If God had instructed humans to do whatever they want, then human choice or fancy would be the basis for value, since doing what we wanted would be obeying God's command and invention. When seeking to determine what has value within the created order, we must seek to find out what God intended for his creation. Without understanding God's creative actions and his intention for his creations, we are at a loss to determine value in any objective sense. The only thing that would be left is a subjective valuation based on the perspective of a creature.

God Declared/Determined What it Means to be Human

In creating humans, God defined humanity. In the same way, by creating stars, God defined what it means to be a star. Had God created humans with other characteristics than those we possess, then what it would mean to be human would be defined concurrent with those alternative characteristics. God's act of creating is the concurrent act of defining the creature.

By Creating Humans

Humans are composed of many qualities. Some of these qualities are such that, when they are removed, the result is no longer a human. Life, for example, is a characteristic of humanity. Where there is no life, there are no humans. Humans are also physical beings. Where there is no matter, there are no humans.

There are also characteristics that do not result in the loss of humanity when a human does not possess them. The characteristic of sight, or being able to see, is common to most humans, but the loss of the ability to see does not mean that humanity is lost. Blind people are still humans, as are blindfolded people. Consciousness is another common characteristic of humanity, but when sleeping, or when consciousness has been lost for other reasons (sedation, a blow to the head, etc.), people do not lose their status as human. If consciousness were a requirement for being human, then we would not be humans while sleeping, and we would have to redefine murder to exclude those killed while sleeping.

While we might like to have an exhaustive list of definitive human characteristics provided by God, we have no such list. We have to determine which characteristics are sufficient for humanity and which are necessary. What we can say without an exhaustive examination of human attributes is that whatever the necessary and sufficient characteristics of humans are, each human possesses them. Characteristics that some humans possess and others do not are neither necessary nor sufficient for humans. While being a mammal may be necessary to being human, having skin pigment is not, since some humans are albinos.

By creating humans, God gave every human the necessary and sufficient attributes of humanity. He also gave various humans other attributes. In creating, God has set the parameters of humanity. In a minimal sense, humans are the collection of necessary and sufficient attributes of humanity. Many humans have attributes beyond this minimal collection. For example, some humans are athletic and have great strength. While great physical strength may be possessed by some humans, it is not necessary for someone to be human. Indeed, many humans are not very strong.

By Giving Creational Mandates

Not only does God determine humanity in an ontological sense, but God determines the function of humanity by mandating roles and behaviors.

God has made both general and specific commands for humans.

> Creational Mandates: Commands issued by God to humanity based on the Creator/creature relationship. These mandates include exercising dominion over creation and procreation.
>
> Covenantal Mandates: Commands issued by God to humanity based on a covenant between God and certain peoples.

Since God's instructions for humanity are the basis for determining value of action, acting human means acting in accordance with God's mandates.

By Providing for and Caring for Humans

God determined what humans would be and what they should do. Beyond the creative action and the instructional mandates, God also provides for and cares for humanity. The world is designed in such a way that humans are able to thrive. God made Earth such that humans could accomplish the mandates he gave to them.

Characteristics of Humanity Declared by God

Imago Dei

> So God created mankind in his own image, in the image of God he created them; male and female he created them. (Gen 1:27)

One of the defining characteristics of Christianity is that God made humans special. We are the only creature described as being made in God's image. While there has been much discussion over exactly what it means to be created in God's image, there is little disagreement that whatever the image of God is, humans possess it.

Early Christians supposed the image of God was that humans walked upright, as opposed to animals, who walked on four legs. Others have suggested that the ability to reason is the image of God. Still others have thought that our ability to relate to one another is the image of God. While I am partial to the idea that reason may be the image of God in humanity, I think it may be our ability, limited as it may be, to transcend the physical world. Although this is not the place to argue for my view of what the *imago dei* is, I will provide a brief description of what I mean before we move on.

Humans are unlike the rest of creation in that, to a limited degree, we are agents who choose how we will react to our circumstances. In other words, human actions are not determined by mere physical processes. I think that the image of God makes sense of our ability to choose at least some of our actions. Physical processes may push us toward certain actions, but we can sometimes choose to take actions contrary to the inclination. I may be hungry, but I can choose not to eat. Or, a more common aspect in the West is that I may not be hungry, but I choose to eat anyway. If humans truly have a degree of free will that transcends the physical world, I think that is as good a candidate for the image of God as any.

Stewards/Representatives to the Created Order

> Then God said, "Let us make mankind in our image, in our likeness, so that they may rule over the fish in the sea and the birds in the sky, over the livestock and all the wild animals, and over all the creatures that move along the ground." (Gen 1:26)

Humans should exercise dominion over creation. In Genesis 1, humans are made in God's image for the purpose of exercising dominion over the other animals. Wherever the animal is located (in the water, in the air, or on the ground) and whether the animals are wild or tame, humans are to rule over them.

The act of ruling has at least two senses. First, it means that human have the authority to use the animals as they see fit. In other words, the rights of the animals are subjected to the authority of humans. Humans may use them for labor or sustenance without consent of the animal. Indeed, the animals may have no ability to consent, but their consent is irrelevant. Authority to utilize animals does not come from the animal, but from the Creator.

Second, ruling means humans have a responsibility for the animals. The created order does not belong to humans. We are merely exercising dominion over it on God's behalf. We have the authority to use animals for our benefit, but that authority is not absolute. In order to properly represent God in creation, we must not only model his power over animals, but also model his character. God is loving and benevolent. He provides and cares for his creation. To model God's character in relation to animal care, we must also be loving and benevolent to the animals under our care. Humans are not free to cause useless suffering or distress to animals.

Beyond animals, this also extends to the rest of the created order. Plant life also should be cared for and used for human benefit without needless destruction and defacing. As we have come to a greater understanding of the interrelationship of the animal and plant kingdoms on our planet, as well as the other natural cycles that affect ecosystems, we need to extend our care beyond specific animals and plants to the underlying systems that support them. In other words, care for all of the created order, in which humans have dominion, is our responsibility. As we have come to see ourselves as part of the global ecosystem, we need to accept responsibility for the proper exercise of our dominion within that ecosystem.

Christians, then, have a responsibility to exercise dominion in a way that honors God. Honoring God in this context means utilizing what he has created for our benefit while treating it in a loving and caring manner. We do not preserve the creation for its own sake, but for God's sake as his representatives.

Social/Community

> The Lord God said, "It is not good for the man to be alone. I will make a helper suitable for him." (Gen 2:18)

Humans are social creatures. We need to relate to others. Many other creatures are also social and thrive only when in groups. Interestingly, in Genesis 2, it seems that the complement to "the man" was given for the purpose of helping him work the ground. This contrasts with Genesis 1, where man and woman are created for exercising dominion.

Without making too much of the differences in the two accounts of creation, humanity, which is complete without community, is nonetheless better in community than in isolation. In addition, gender differences are not necessary to humanity, yet humanity is better with them. Procreation, another mandate, cannot be fulfilled without the social aspect of human existence.

God created humans with a need for one another. He also gave mandates that cannot be accomplished without social interactions and relationships. The social aspect of humans cannot and must not be diminished, but should be viewed in relationship to the other aspects of humanity. Humans are creatures that are better in community than in isolation. A human can exist in the absence of other humans, but that is not a good way for humans to exist.

Social relationships are to aid in accomplishing the other tasks God mandated for us. They are not to replace those tasks. In other words, the social aspect of humanity is not the goal, in and of itself. It is an aid to accomplishing the dominion and filling of the Earth.

GOD'S CREATED PURPOSES FOR HUMANITY

Glorify God

The Westminster Catechism is famous for the answer to its first question. Christians around the world use a version of this catechism in the rearing of their families. The first question asks what is the chief and highest end of man, or humanity? The answer provided is to glorify God, and to fully enjoy him forever. One of the purposes humans fulfill is bringing glory to God. God is glorified by his creatures. Humans, by their very existence, glorify God. They may glorify God intentionally or unintentionally.

Glorifying God: Scriptural Basis

This section will examine a few passages undergirding the conception that humanity should bring glory to God. The first section will examine passages indicating that God created humanity for the purpose of receiving glory. The next section will examine passages indicating that God has commanded us to glorify him.

In Isaiah, we see a direct proclamation that God has created humans, particularly his people, for his glory.

> I will say to the north, "Give them up!" and to the south, "Do not hold them back." Bring my sons from afar and my daughters from the ends of the earth—everyone who is called by my name, whom I created for my glory, whom I formed and made. (Isa 43:6–7)

God takes credit for forming humans and tells us that they are for the purpose of glorifying him. This is the most direct passage that we have to indicate glorifying God as a purpose of humanity.

The next passage to examine is from David. This passage is after the people have brought wealth to donate to the building of the temple. David is humbled that he and others are able to take part in the funding of the temple.

> David praised the Lord in the presence of the whole assembly, saying, "Praise be to you, Lord, the God of our father Israel, from everlasting to everlasting. Yours, Lord, is the greatness and the power and the glory and the majesty and the splendor, for everything in heaven and earth is yours. Yours, Lord, is the kingdom; you are exalted as head over all. Wealth and honor come from you; you are the ruler of all things. In your hands are strength and power to exalt and give strength to all. Now, our God, we give you thanks, and praise your glorious name." (1 Chr 29:10–13)

In this song of praise, David acknowledges the greatness of God. He notes that everything belongs to God, that God is powerful, and that God is the ruler of all. On the basis of who God is, David indicates that the people will praise God and give thanks. David seems to think that humans should praise God based on his greatness.

Peter also indicates that God should be glorified in everything that people do. In his first epistle he tells the churches that they should act as representatives of God. If anyone speaks, they should do so as one who speaks the very words of God. If anyone serves, they should do so with the strength God provides, so that in all things God may be praised through Jesus Christ. To him be the glory and the power for ever and ever. Amen (1 Pet 4:11). Peter tells the churches that God should be praised in all things. If all of a creature's actions have an obligatory aspect of glorifying God, it is a reasonable assumption that the purpose of the creature is to glorify God. Paul also uses this line of thinking. Humans should bring God glory in all of their actions, public and private.

> So whether you eat or drink or whatever you do, do it all for the glory of God. (1 Cor 10:31)

Again, if everything people do should be such that God is glorified, it seems reasonable that at least part of the purpose of humanity's creation was to glorify God.

In addition to passages that indicate a purpose of humanity is God's glorification, numerous passages command people to glorify God. If part of what it means to be a human is derived from the mandates God gives to humanity, then it follows that what God commands people to do is part of their purpose. Since God commands people to glorify him, the purpose of humanity, at least in part, is glorifying God.

The psalmist directs all people to glorify God. All nations are instructed to follow his command. This is a passage that shows the universal nature of command to glorify God.

> Ascribe to the Lord, all you families of nations, ascribe to the Lord glory and strength. Ascribe to the Lord the glory due his name; bring an offering and come into his courts. (Ps 96:7–8)

God is due glory and everyone is obligated to give what is due. The psalmist provides an open command and invitation to everyone.

In Revelation we have another universal command to glorify God. In this passage, the command comes from an angel and is addressed to everyone.

> Then I saw another angel flying in midair, and he had the eternal gospel to proclaim to those who live on the earth—to every nation, tribe, language and people. He said in a loud voice, "Fear God and give him glory, because the hour of his judgment has come. Worship him who made the heavens, the earth, the sea and the springs of water." (Rev 14:6–7)

With God's righteous judgment at hand, the people are told to worship and glorify God.

Isaiah also commands people to worship God. People all over the earth are to bring God a new song. They are to sing for joy and raise their voices for God's glory.

> Sing to the Lord a new song, his praise from the ends of the earth, you who go down to the sea, and all that is in it, you islands, and all who live in them. Let the wilderness and its towns raise their voices; let the settlements where Kedar lives rejoice. Let the people of Sela sing for joy; let them shout from the mountaintops. Let them give glory to the Lord and proclaim his praise in the islands. (Isa 42:10–12)

God commands all people to praise him and bring him glory.

Since God's command to humanity is not restricted to a particular group of people in a special relationship with God, the best way to see the commands to glorify God is as a universal imperative. Everyone everywhere is commanded to glorify God for who he is and for what he has done. In addition, since we have passages that indicate part of God's purpose in creating humanity was for his own glorification, we have a twofold reason for accepting a purpose of human existence is to glorify God.

Glorifying God: Relationship with God

God is glorified when his creatures enter into loving relationships with him. Humans are created with a degree of autonomy. We often use our freedom for evil and rebellion. God has sought to allow humans to be in a proper relationship with him since the garden. In order for us to be in proper relationship with God, we must submit to his authority. We must recognize that we are creatures, not the Creator. We must respect the limitations of humanity and not seek to usurp God's prerogatives.

In the garden, Adam and Eve sought to have knowledge that they were not permitted to have. In violating God's parameters, they sought to be more than they were created to be. They tried to appropriate something that God had not intended for them to have. The Tree of the Knowledge of Good and Evil gave them knowledge, but not in the way that they expected. They knew what good and evil were because they had committed an evil action.

God expelled them from the garden and brought a curse on the land as a punishment. The rest of the Bible is the recurring theme of God bringing people into relationship with himself. God takes the initiative, and people respond and relate to God properly for a while before falling away. God brings judgment and offers restoration. The cycle repeats in the Old Testament and is completed in the sacrificial death of the Messiah in the New Testament.

Jesus tells his disciples that, by being properly related to him, and through him to the Father, God is glorified.

> If you remain in me and my words remain in you, ask whatever you wish, and it will be done for you. This is to my Father's glory, that you bear much fruit, showing yourselves to be my disciples. (John 15:7–8)

Somehow God is brought glory when his creatures relate to him properly.

Glorifying God: Dominion Over Creation

God created humans to exercise dominion over his creation. When we function as we should, God is glorified. Part of Adam's function was to work the garden. Before the fall, we see that work and responsibility were part of God's intention for humanity. Working with something for the purpose of taking care of it is exercising authority over it or conforming it to the will of the workers. After the fall, when God banishes Adam, he commands Adam to work the ground from which he came. However, the ground will be more difficult to work now because of Adam's sin.

Properly understood, exercising dominion over the earth is working the earth to produce food for its inhabitants and making it all that it can be for God's own glory. Millard Erickson writes, "The exercise of dominion is a consequence of the image of God. Humanity is to gain an understanding and control of the creation, developing it to its ultimate potential for its own good and for God."[4] We might argue about where the limits of production and exploitation lie, and that is an important discussion to have. We might also argue about what states are the most glorious or the best state the creation can be in to give God glory. The purpose of this section is not to sketch out the parameters of those arguments, but to generally show that dominion of the creation by mankind glorifies God.

---

4. Erickson, *Christian Theology*, 535.

When humans work the creation and cause it to produce for sustenance, God is glorified and his providential provision for his people is shown. When humans preserve, improve, or edify the environment, God is glorified and the beauty of his creation is on display. When humans exercise dominion, they show God's beauty and power on his behalf. God is glorified when his image bearers display the powers he has given them to manage his creation.

Glorifying God: Relating to Others in Community

God created humans to be in relationship with one another in community, and he is glorified when we have community as he intended. God as Trinity is the perfect example of loving communion. Within the Trinity is perfect love, admiration, submission, unity, and purpose. Human relationship will never be as complete as the intra-Trinitarian relationships are, but they can mirror them to some degree.

God determined that it was not good for Adam to be alone. He created Eve as a suitable companion and helper. Humans have a need to relate to one another socially. The basic building block of society is the complementary model of human relationship depicted in Genesis 2: man and woman living and working together and producing children to fill the earth and to have dominion over it.

To have a properly functioning relationship at the most basic level, the man and woman should love each other. That love should be the giving of one for the other. They should also admire each other, recognizing the traits and abilities possessed by their complementary partner. The man and the woman should submit to one another. Neither should dominate the other; out of respect and love they each should be willing to defer to the other as the situation determines. They should be united in mutual commitment to one another. This unity should be strong enough to withstand the storms and trials of life. Finally, they should share the same purpose. The goal and intent for the male-female relationship is the successful completion of the task God set before them.

Beyond the basic family unit, children are an important part of the equation. The parents should model all of the aforementioned characteristics and should teach their children how to do this themselves. Expanding further leads to extended family. Each basic family unit should model the characteristics for each other family. Continue to expand the sphere of influence and we have groups of extended families that are either distantly related or unrelated. In this community the larger family units can model proper functioning for everyone surrounding them.

God is glorified when his people model the example relationships found within the Trinity. The more closely we approach the way the members of the Trinity relate to one another, the better our own society will function and the more glory we will bring to God. "You were bought at a price. Therefore honor God with your bodies" (1 Cor 6:20). We honor God with our bodies in a number of ways, not the least of which is in the marriage relationship. The man and woman become one flesh and, to some degree, this single flesh brings God honor. This honor must be in the context of the marriage relationship. The marriage relationship as the basic unit of society begins the process that echoes outward into the larger community. God is honored by men and women, their children, their extended families, and eventually their communities. As the basic family unit increases its honor for God, the more clearly its echoes reverberate outward into the creation. Human community should seek to model the relationships found within the Trinity.

Finding Satisfaction in God

God is glorified in the actions of humans without needing the person to acknowledge God. All creatures bring glory to God in that way, by their very existence and their functioning as they ought. Sentient beings also glorify God by acknowledging their submission to God and finding satisfaction in their actions. God is glorified by those who refuse to acknowledge him in their actions and accomplishments but, since they do not acknowledge God, they do not glorify God by submitting to him. God is further glorified (a second level of glory) when those who acknowledge and accept him act with the realization that what they are doing is for God's glory and find satisfaction in their own obedience and submission.

Those who refuse to give the second level of glory to God deny him what is rightfully his. Instead of glorifying God by finding satisfaction in him, they glorify themselves. Taking pride in their own accomplishments, they assert independence rather than acknowledging dependence on God. They are guilty of depriving God what is due him and taking it for themselves.

Finding Satisfaction in God: Scriptural Basis

Many passages of Scripture indicate that humans should take delight in what God provides. We read passages thanking God for deliverance, safety, and provision. While it is proper to acknowledge God's care, we should also acknowledge and find satisfaction, or contentment, in our own service to God.

Wisdom literature provides guidance for living well. In Proverbs, we find some passages which tell the reader of consequences for certain behaviors or attitudes. Fearing or respecting God is a positive attitude and has beneficial consequences. "The fear of the Lord leads to life; then one rests content, untouched by trouble" (Prov 19:23). Respecting God brings people to contentment by bringing them to follow God's commands. In addition, the attitude of reverence for God allows people to properly attribute glory to God rather than to themselves.

The Psalms also provide encouragement for those seeking to know how to relate to God in the proper manner. Although they are poetic, they provide the idea of a natural consequence for behavior. When people relate to God as they should, they have the opportunity to be in God's presence. Those in rebellion against God do not find themselves close to God. Those who are close to God find life and bliss. "You make known to me the path of life; you will fill me with joy in your presence, with eternal pleasures at your right hand" (Ps 16:11).

In addition to the benefits of being in God's presence, those who focus on God, rather than on themselves, find that God gives them the things they long for. "Take delight in the Lord, and he will give you the desires of your heart" (Ps 37:4).

Finding contentment, satisfaction, or delight in God allows our attitude to function the way God intended. Focusing on God and locating our satisfaction in him, rather than on ourselves or our situations, orients our desires toward the giver of life and the single unchanging power in the universe. Since God is unchanging, we have access to a stable foundation for our contentment, satisfaction, and delight.

Finding Satisfaction in God: Submitting to God's Will

When humans find satisfaction in God, and submit to his will, they humble themselves. Humility and submission are the proper attitudes when relating to God, but not always the easiest of attitudes for humans to take.

We like to think we are more, or should be more, than we are. We look at our accomplishments and are proud. We extrapolate our successes and begin to believe that there is nothing we cannot do. Archimedes wrote that he could move the world with a lever and a place to stand. In Genesis 11, humans boast they can build a tower to reach the heavens. In modern times, we often see people who, after having some success, make grand boasts. We sometimes speak of people "starting to believe their own press releases" when we see someone who's confidence and pride are out of control.

Because humans have some power and some transcendence over the world, we can accomplish great things. The power can go to our heads, and we often forget about the source of our own strength and intellect. Just as the sin of the garden was a desire to be more than what humans were created to be, we often seek to usurp God's role and assert our own power.

God is not threatened by human accomplishment; rather, he is glorified by it. God's plans for humanity are more grand than we can fathom. When we fail to acknowledge God and find satisfaction in ourselves or our accomplishments, we are robbing God of glory. Since all glory is rightfully his, we become thieves. Keeping the glory for ourselves, in an attempt to become more like God, we do not come closer to him. Taking God's glory for ourselves sets us in opposition to him. The more we take, the further we move away from him.

When we submit ourselves to God and bring him all the glory, we are brought closer to him. The more we empty ourselves and rely on God, the more he fills us and glorifies us. Jesus, being the example of this counterintuitive idea, emptied himself and was exalted.

> In your relationships with one another, have the same mindset as Christ Jesus: Who, being in very nature God, did not consider equality with God something to be used to his own advantage; rather, he made himself nothing by taking the very nature of a servant, being made in human likeness. And being found in appearance as a man, he humbled himself by becoming obedient to death—even death on a cross! Therefore God exalted him to the highest place and gave him the name that is above every name, that at the name of Jesus every knee should bow, in heaven and

on earth and under the earth, and every tongue acknowledge that
Jesus Christ is Lord, to the glory of God the Father. (Phil 2:5–11)

Becoming closer to and more like God is achieved, not by denying God the glory he is due, but by attributing it to him and humbling ourselves.

It is no wonder that the psalmist was puzzled by nations opposing and raging against God. When we seek to amass power and glory on our own, without regard for God, we become enemies of God. Stealing God's glory takes us further away from the source of life and power. Instead of becoming stronger and more like God, we become weaker and less like him. When we follow Jesus' example, and are obedient and humble, God increases our power. As Christians become more sanctified, we become more like God. Those who seek to become more like God by stealing from him are going in the wrong direction, since you cannot take from God by force what he gives freely through obedience.

Finding Satisfaction in God: By Exercising Dominion

Managing God's creation as he intended is another way to bring glory to God. God is glorified when humans exercise dominion over the creation, but when humans exercise that dominion within his parameters, God's glory increases.

What do I mean when I claim we should exercise dominion within God's parameters? I mean that there are certain ways of utilizing the creation that are acceptable. Dominion according to God's parameters does not mean humans can do whatever they want to with the creation. As representatives of the Creator, we must exercise dominion in a manner consistent with God's character. This project is not a work of Christian ethics, so I will not suggest specific practices for an ethic of dominion. I will, however, sketch the theological parameters within which an ethic of dominion could be built. We need such an ethic.

Humans finding satisfaction in dominion means demonstrating God's character to the creation. Humans should bring forth from the creation that which it was designed to produce. Crops and livestock are the examples from Genesis. Since the writers of Scripture lived in a world that was much closer to agriculture than is most of the developed world, we should not be surprised that food crops and livestock are given as examples.

I will present three aspects of God's character to build an ethic of dominion around. These aspects are love, provision, and protection.

God loves. God expresses that love within the Trinity and to the creation. When humans exercise dominion, they should do so with a love for what God loves. That means they should themselves love God and love his creation. Loving God will mean submitting to his will and finding satisfaction in him. Loving the creation will mean utilizing the creation without abusing it. In agriculture, this will mean producing the best of what the Earth can produce without destroying it. Crops should be produced to maximize yield without depleting the soil. Quality foods that provide good nutrition for humans should be produced without destroying other parts of the environment. Animal production should not cause suffering. Love for the creation does not destroy a portion of it to provide for another.

God provides for his creation. He makes the rains fall and the sun shine. When humans exercise dominion, they should do so in a way that provides for all aspects of the creation. Humans must produce food to live. But the production of food for humans must also account for the needs of the other parts of the creation as well. We understand that ecosystems can be disrupted. Overuse and/or failure to provide what is taken out of a system can cause it to fail. The provisions we must make are not only for humans. We must make provision for the other parts of the ecosystems as well. Provision for the ecosystems may come in the form of planting crops that build the soil but may not be for human consumption. It may come in the form of allowing a farmed area to rest. The best of what we know about the needs of humans and the environment should be taken into consideration as we attempt to produce what is needed for both.

God protects what is his. When humans exercise dominion, they should do so in a way that protects all aspects of the creation. Humans should protect themselves from danger. We should also protect our crops and livestock. In addition, we should protect the ecosystems that allow the Earth to produce. We have a duty to provide protection from whatever threat comes about. Threats may be wild animals, pests, or other humans.

Ethics is a complicated field. We have to address conflicting priorities from time to time. A Christian ethic of dominion will help us understand conflicts that arise in life as it relates to exercising dominion over the creation. When humans exercise dominion properly, they show obedience to their Creator and his commands. God is glorified in the submission and obedience of his creatures as it relates to dominion.

Created for Relationship

Finding Satisfaction in God: By Experiencing Community as God Intended

When humans experience community, God is glorified. When humans submit to God's will in their community, God is further glorified. Throughout the Bible, humans are called to live in a community that honors God, but they stray and rebel. The inability of people to live in a proper relationship to both God and one another is solved by Jesus. The formation of God's people, the church, is the solution to the problem of inadequate communities.

Within the church, the intra-Trinitarian relationship is modeled by her members. Modeling those characteristics (love, admiration, submission, unity, and purpose) are done intentionally and within the framework that God has provided. In the church, or God's family, we find satisfaction in submitting to God's will for our community.

God is glorified in the church in two ways. First, as the church grows numerically, more people live and find satisfaction in God's family. As more people become part of the church, more people begin to live in the community that God intended. They begin to find satisfaction in God, and he is further glorified.

Second, as the church grows in maturity (sanctification), the members more clearly exhibit love, admiration, submission, unity, and purpose. The Christian life is a process. It takes time to mature. As the church becomes better at living as God's family, God is further glorified.

Living Fully

> The thief comes only to steal and kill and destroy; I have come that they may have life, and have it to the full. (John 10:10)

When people relate to God as they were intended to, they experience life as God has planned. That means they will have life to the full. In the West, many have wrongly used this verse to support the idea that a faithful Christian life will be materially prosperous and physically healthy. Jesus, however, was speaking of having life to the full in the context of sheep and the good shepherd.

The Christian has the fullness of life because of the relationship to God and the role that he or she has to play in their work (exercising dominion) and in the church. Fullness of life is not simply a way of talking about a life beyond this life, though it includes that idea. Fullness of life is also not just speaking about intangible spiritual blessings, though it includes that idea also. Fullness of life is referring to the totality of human experience in properly relating to God and the creation and is functioning properly within the creation.

Living Fully: Scriptural Basis

Living a full life, as Jesus explains in John 10:10, will mean being one of Jesus' sheep. He speaks of his sheep hearing his voice and following him. In the larger passage, he makes clear that those who are not following him do not belong to him. Jesus' followers are the church. The proper way to relate to Jesus and the Father is by being part of the church.

In Matthew, we also find Jesus telling people that when their lives are properly ordered, they will have the things that they need. There is no need to worry about the necessities of life, God knows what people need, and he is good. "But seek first the kingdom of God and his righteousness, and all these things will be added to you" (Matt 6:33). When you do what you are supposed to do, God will ensure that you are cared for. This is similar to the idea of the good shepherd caring for his own.

Paul also lends support to the idea that a full life is found in properly relating to God. In Romans, he discusses how Christians are aided in life by God's providential action and the intervention of the spirit. "And we know that for those who love God all things work together for good, for those who are called according to his purpose" (Rom 8:28). When we don't know what to do, God is there. When we feel separated from God, Paul reminds us that nothing can separate us from Christ. When we are being persecuted, Paul tells us that we are allied with God, who cannot fail.

Similarly, in Philippians, Paul again shows how God provides what he needs. In this case, Paul is finding contentment, not in his circumstances, but in God. "I can do all things through him who strengthens me" (Phil 4:13). Paul learned to live with much or little, as far as material possessions are concerned. He relied on God for accomplishing his task. Paul's life was full, even though sometimes his stomach was not. Even when he lacked material support, he had the strength and comfort that comes from God, which was sufficient.

Created for Relationship

Living Fully: A Proper Relationship with God Allows for a Full Life

When we are properly related to God, that is, when we are in Christ, we have the fullness of life. All humans, like the rest of the creation, have a relationship to God as creature to Creator. As a sentient being, humans also have a behavioral aspect of relating to God. That is, we are either obedient or rebellious. Our sin places us against God and in a state of rebellion. No human is fully obedient to God, and all humans rebel against him.

Through the gospel, humans can find a restored relationship with God. They become obedient and no longer rebels. When we are no longer against God, we find his love and grace as abundant provision. But there is more to a full life. In Christ, we are not simply creatures who were formerly rebellious and now obedient. The Bible indicates that we become God's children.

In one sense, everyone is a child of God. God is the Creator and all humans are created in his image. But Christians are told that we are also accepted as heirs with Christ. We are adopted into God's family and now can relate to him as a loving father. Being part of God's family is a wonderful thing. It means that we can ask for things with an expectation of good. Jesus provides a wonderful example of God's goodness in Matthew.

> Or which one of you, if his son asks him for bread, will give him a stone? Or if he asks for a fish, will give him a serpent? If you then, who are evil, know how to give good gifts to your children, how much more will your Father who is in heaven give good things to those who ask him! (Matt 7:9–11)

Adoption, an often-overlooked doctrine, gives a powerful expectation of good things from our Father in heaven. Since God has no limitation on what he can give us, we can know that he will bring us the good things he desires for us to have. Our life will be filled with the things that are according to his good will for us.

Living Fully: Proper Dominion Allows for a Full Life

When we exercise the dominion we are tasked with, living in the proper way, we will experience a full life. Humans are diverse and different. We like different foods, music, and activities, and have a countless host of other preferences.

In our diversity, God has called us to serve in different capacities. Some of us he has called into fields that require constant interpersonal relationships. Others he has called to work alone, or with few people. Some are called to work the land, and others are called to work animals. Some are called to academic study, and others are called to work with their hands.

In all the various ways that God calls his people to exercise dominion over the creation, we should seek to align our lives with what God has called us to accomplish. When we are aligned with God's particular calling for our lives, we will find more satisfaction in our work. Romans 8:28 notes the way that God works things together, but it also indicates that we should also align ourselves with his purpose. The ordering of things to good is dependent on God's purpose for those things. In other words, something is good if it is aligned with God's plans and purposes. It makes sense that our work should be aligned with God's purpose for us. Our lives will not only be full in the sense that we have expectations of blessings from God, but our lives will also be full in the sense that we will be performing according to our individual design. Our fullness will come not only from the accomplishing tasks, but from knowing that the tasks we are accomplishing are what God has intended and designed us to do.

Living Fully: A Proper Relationship to God's Community Allows for a Full Life

The final aspect of having a full life is in the relationship to the community God has intended for people; that community is the church. The church is special to God. It is the place where his people come to worship him and share life with one another. As social creatures, we need the interaction with other humans. In the church we find interaction, not only with other humans, but with family. We are siblings in the family of God.

The importance of viewing fellow Christians as siblings will be examined later in the work, but for now we should realize that the sibling relationship was a very valuable and treasured relationship in the ancient world. In many ways, the concept that "blood is thicker than water" can be seen in the devotion siblings had in the ancient world.

To demonstrate how life is made more full in the church, I will quickly examine four aspects. First, Christians find comfort in the church. Living life with a family that is able to relate to our struggles and hardships is comforting. When we have loss, the church is able to mourn with us. When we have joy, the church can rejoice with us. When we need an encouraging word, our brothers and sisters have the opportunity to soothe us. The church provides comfort for her members.

Second, Christians find wisdom in the church. Knowledge is important, but it is vital to know how to apply the things we know to the various situations in which we find ourselves. The church provides access across generations. Younger people have older members who can give accounts of their own experiences and share their wisdom. The love the church has for one another provides reasons to share. The church provides wisdom for her members.

Third, Christians find guidance in the church. We often struggle with indecision or difficult choices. Sometimes we seek God, but our own situations and anxiety cloud our ability to clearly discern his leading. Sometimes, and perhaps often, God provides the guidance we seek through our brothers and sisters in the church. Apart from wisdom of others, God providentially moves his people to provide guidance we need. By being in close relationship with other believers, we increase the opportunity to receive guidance through God's people. The church provides guidance for her members.

Finally, Christians receive blessing through the church. Some blessing we receive by simply having relationships with others in the church. Other blessings are arranged by God through his people. Churches can provide food for those in need. In the Bible, we find that lodging was a way Christians blessed other Christians, and it can be that way today as well. Churches can help meet financial or emotional needs. Through the church, families can get help with projects or even simply help to care for children. There are many ways that life is made more full through being part of God's family. The church provides blessings for her members.

Chapter Three

Created with Needs

HUMANS HAVE NEEDS

Humans are needy. We need food. We need water. We need sleep and shelter. Beyond those needs, we must have meaningful relationships where we feel accepted. We also need tasks to give our life purpose. In Clifton Williams's book *Existential Reasons for Belief in God*, he notes several types of needs that humans have. He uses the existence of those needs as justification for a rational belief in God. I propose that humans have needs for autonomy and for dependence. In other words, people have certain existential needs to feel like they are in control and that they can direct themselves in this world to some degree. Humans don't like to feel like they are simply puppets. We want to think that our decisions matter, that they are meaningful.

In addition, humans also have a need for security and belonging. Ultimately, although we want to do some things by ourselves, we don't really want isolation. We want to be part of something larger than ourselves—part of something that allows us to be vulnerable and accepted. Humans need relationships with others.

Because humans have these needs, and because humans were created by God, it is reasonable to believe that we have some way to satisfy those needs. The way humans can find satisfaction for our needs will be discussed in a later chapter.

Created with Needs

Human Needs are Real

God created us and we exist. We exist in the physical world and our bodies demand food, water, and sleep, among other things. Not all of our needs are physical, but certainly we have physical needs that we must meet. We do not deny that we need to eat food, though we may do just fine with much less food. We do not deny that we need water, and we go to great lengths to make sure we have it. We try to sleep on a regular basis, and if we don't we suffer the consequences. Humans have certain needs as a consequence of being a physical being. We don't question the reality of our physical needs.

We also have emotional needs, but those are more difficult to quantify. We have certain needs for relationships. My wife has a need to talk much more than I do. My daughters have the same need. When we have been away from people we care about, we desire to spend time with them. The emotional needs of connection and sharing are genuine. Though they are not physical needs, they need to be met in a similar way to food, water, and sleep.

We may claim that we don't need to eat. But failing to eat will eventually lead to death. We may claim that we do not need water. But failing to drink will lead to death in just a few days. We may claim that we don't need sleep, but just a few short days without sleep bring severe consequences. Our physical needs, when they are not met, exhibit consequences in a very real and dramatic way.

Our emotional needs are no less important, but they manifest much differently when they are not met. People may live alone for a long period of time. People mourn the loss of a loved one for a long time without ever being able to see them again. Sometimes people have severe emotional reactions, and other times they don't. This does not mean that the needs are any less real; it simply means that problems that arise from failing to meet emotional needs manifest differently than physical needs.

But human needs are real. Denying that we have either physical or emotional needs is foolish. Part of being human is having certain physical and emotional needs. Having needs is not a defect. Having needs is part of our design as human beings. God knows that we have these needs. He created us with those needs.

Human Needs Were Determined by God

> We are designed to find our meaning and identity in relation to, and only in relation to, God.[1]

Humanity did not create itself. Even for those who see the origin of humanity as a completely naturalistic process, humans are not responsible for their own creation. For the naturalist, our ancestors are responsible for humanity because they survived, and their descendants eventually became us. But even in this view, our ancestors did not create us, they became us. A blind force ultimately stands behind the origin of life and is responsible for it.

Christian theology does not allow for such an unguided and purposeless creation. God, who is ultimately responsible for creating the universe, including humanity, is ordered and purposeful in his creation. Humans were created with a purpose, and they were also created with needs. Human needs are not accidental, God did not make a mistake. Human needs were designed by God to allow us to fulfill his purpose in our lives.

The good news is that we don't get hungry, thirsty, and sleepy for no reason. God could have created humanity in such a way that one or more of these needs did not apply. Imagine what life would be like if we never hungered, or imagine how much you could get done if you didn't have a need for sleep. Presumably, God could have created us so that we never needed sleep. Without speculating too much on what life without sleep might be like or whether we should want such a thing, the fact is that God created us with a need for sleep. God knew before he created us that we would need to sleep, and he knew the limitations that fulfilling that need would place upon us. He also knew that we would need to eat and need to drink, and the limitations that those needs place upon us. He created us with those needs anyway. Somehow, having those physical needs is important for the human experience.

We can speculate on the many reasons why God may have chosen to give us the particular needs that he did. Perhaps having physical needs is a witness to the fact that God is our Creator. Perhaps because we have needs that have to be met on a regular basis, our attention is drawn toward God, who provides for those needs. Maybe having to meet needs on a regular basis is one way that God reminds us that we are not divine. Perhaps we could think of a hundred other reasons why having physical needs is beneficial

---

1. Grenz, *Community of God*, 132.

for humanity as God intended it. The same is true for emotional needs. For whatever reason, God intended humans to have needs for interaction with others.

Regardless of why God created humans with needs, he did. God is responsible for humanity having needs, and there's no way that he can get out of being responsible for the needs. Since God is also a good God, he has made sure that human needs are able to be fulfilled. In fact, the Bible praises God for meeting the needs of his people. Humans have genuine needs that are designed by God and are part of being human.

Human Needs Can be Fulfilled/Met

Imagine a world where humans exist and are hungry, but there is nothing to eat. Imagine a world where humans exist and are thirsty, but there is nothing to drink. Imagine a world where humans exist and they are tired and sleepy, but sleep is not to be found. What kind of world would this be? It certainly would not be a world that was hospitable to humanity. The world we live in is not that kind of world. God created humanity with physical and emotional needs, and he created the means to meet those needs.

Our world has food sources and water to meet our nutritional demands. Humans are able to find rest and sleep to rejuvenate their bodies. The other emotional needs that we have are also able to be met in the company of friends and relatives. God has created a world in which humans are able to satisfy the needs they have.

It's reasonable to assume that any genuine need humans have can be met. If God is good, as the Bible claims that he is, and he created humans with needs, then it is reasonable to assume that God provided a way to meet those needs. That is not to say that anything any person desires has the ability to be met or should be met. Needs are not identical to desires, and should not be confused with them. They are the aspects of human existence that, when unmet, diminishes the human person. If God created us with needs and failed to provide a way for those needs to be met, his character could be called into question.

The good news is that, although humans have real needs, those needs were created by a good God who also provided a way to satisfy them. In the following section, I am going to discuss two categories of human needs: autonomy and dependence.

Human Autonomy

Humans feel like we have some form of control over our lives and of ourselves. At different times, this control may be diminished to very small levels, but we need to feel autonomous to some degree. Human need for autonomy is manifested in three ways: self-direction, significance, and genuineness.

Need for Self-Direction

Imagine for a moment that you exist as a character in a story. You get up in the morning and go through your routine. Perhaps you take a shower and get ready for your day. You go to work, accomplishing tasks that you believe will advance your career. Maybe you go to lunch with some colleagues and discuss plans for the weekend or for the next quarter. You finish your day and go home to your family. The next day you get up and do it all over again.

Now imagine that your character becomes aware that he or she is simply a character in some book. That all of the decisions you remembered making throughout your entire life, and in fact all of the decisions you're making, even to this moment, are not your own. Some unknown author has created you and your entire life story. Everything you think you've done, you did, not because you necessarily chose to, but because someone else decided you would.

I suspect many of us would not feel genuine if that were the case. We would feel like something is false. Even if we decided to do all of the things that we remember doing and all of the things that we were currently doing, it would seem like they were not our own choices. Maybe they weren't. Maybe our choices were simply the byproduct of the author's choice. Nevertheless, if we had an awareness that our life was like the life of a character in some novel, we might not be happy about it. I think the reason is that we seem to think that we actually make decisions, and that our own decisions are meaningful and actually our own. When I decided what to eat for breakfast, although my choices may be limited, my English muffin with eggs and cheese is my decision. If the choice of breakfast food was actually mine, then there is also an implicit understanding that had I chosen to eat something else, I could have.

Created with Needs

Without arguing the merits of whether or not we have free will, at least free will to that degree, most humans seem to have some need for self-directedness. We want our decisions to originate somewhere in ourselves. We don't like the idea that we might be robots or we might be characters in some novel. We want to feel like we are directing our life to some degree. We realize that there may be many restricting factors in the choices that we make. Certainly, issues like our health, our bank account, or the particular part of the world that we live in restrict the choices that we can make. But that does not mean we don't have any freedom at all. Sometimes when we seem to be the most limited by constraining factors, it is the time when we most yearn to make one simple choice that we feel is our own.

At times, children will go to great lengths to express autonomy. I can remember times as a child when I felt like I had no control over my life. In those times, in whatever small way possible, I wanted to exert some control over some small portion of my life. We see examples of this when children refuse to eat foods that they may otherwise love because they feel like their life is out of control; they feel like they have no choice in anything. Their food, the things they will put into their body, is one area where they have some control, and they want to exercise that control.

God understands our needs for autonomy. In the book of Genesis, when God created Adam and set him in the garden, he gave him a degree of freedom. "The Lord God took the man and put him in the Garden of Eden to work it and to care for it and the Lord God commanded the man you are free to eat from any tree in the garden but you must not eat from the tree of the knowledge of good and evil for when you eat of it you will surely die" (Gen 2:15–17).

God creates the man and places him in a garden. Adam is there to work the garden and to take care of it. He is also free to eat from the garden as he has need and want. There are restrictions on his freedom. God tells him of a certain tree from which he should not eat, but there are presumably many other trees from which Adam is free to eat. So even in the narrative of the first human, we see God granting Adam a degree of autonomy in his choices.

Adam seems to have free reign in choosing how to work and how to take care of the garden. We have no way of knowing what kinds of work needed to be done in the garden. We have no way of knowing what choices Adam made in taking care of the garden. But it seems that Adam did have some kind of choice and autonomy in making his choices. Looking on, it seems that some time must have passed with Adam working the garden alone in order for God to say that it was no longer good for Adam to be alone.

In the very beginning of the Bible's portrayal of humanity, we find that humans, and in particular Adam, have a degree of autonomy. Adam's autonomy seems to be manifested, at least in part, by the way he chooses to care for and work the garden and with respect to eating from the garden. In the first chapters of Genesis, we see God meeting the human need for autonomy. Adam has some degree of self-direction immediately after being created by God.

Need for Significance and Genuineness

Although the ability to make autonomous choices is important, it is not sufficient. It's not enough that we have the ability to make our own choices, those choices also need to be significant. Choice for choice's sake is not good enough.

Humans want our choices to be our own. It's not enough that we are able to make a choice; we need to believe that the choice originated within ourselves to some degree. In the example of the author making the choices for his or her character, we can see the frustration that arises from choices with questionable origin.

One way that humans can have their need for making real choices affirmed is by discussing the process of choice selection and deliberation with others. When we talk about the way we came to a decision, we feel better about our control in the matter, that we actually made the decision. If our decisions come to us without any deliberation or any thought, then we may begin to question if we are actually making our own decisions. For some reason, we seem to value our decision-making when we have deliberation related to making the decision. Talking with others about our lives, the decisions we are making, and the consequences of those decisions is affirming. This helps us to believe that we really did make the decisions for reasons that we may or may not be willing to admit.

Another way that humans can affirm their ability to make real choices is based on the consequences of their choices. Many of us have wished that we could go back and change a particular choice we made in the past. If only we had known! The older we get, the more times we wish that we could go back and change some decision that we made. Perhaps we would have studied harder for a test. Perhaps we would have heeded a warning from a loved one or friend. Perhaps you would have taken a right turn at Albuquerque. Whatever the choice, there are things that we regret because we did not like the consequence.

Other times we think of choices that we believe would have led to better circumstances. We may think about the way our life would have been different if we had made a different choice, or we reflect on the choice we did make and see how it was ultimately what we should have done. In either case, the decisions we make, our later reflection on those decisions, and the consequences reinforce the idea that we actually made a real choice.

Summation of Autonomous Needs

Humans have needs that mark us out as individuals. We have needs that make us feel independent from the world around us. Although some of these needs are best met in the context of others, we still feel like we need to be autonomous. We recognize that our autonomy is not absolute, and that our choices are limited by a whole host of constraining factors. But constrained as we are, we do feel like we need to express ourselves and our individuality.

Since God created us this way, he has provided a way for us to fulfill those needs. We live in a world where we make our own choices. We have to live with the consequences of those choices whether they are good or bad. We have memories of the choices we made and the reasons we have for making those choices. Those memories help us to believe that we really made these choices ourselves. We have the ability to work toward goals, and this allows us to have significance or some semblance of it.

HUMAN DEPENDENCE

Although we have burning desires for autonomy, we also have desires to belong and to be part of something. We want to be unique and self-directed, but we don't want to be out there all by ourselves. We are social beings. We long for security and for being part of a group. We want to be strong and independent, and at the same time we also have a need to be vulnerable and accepted. We want to know that we are not going through life alone. When I get sad, I want to know that others get sad and get through it. When I feel like I can't go on, I want to know that others have gone on. When I see someone being treated unfairly, I want to believe in justice.

These types of needs are expressed within a social context and fulfilled with relationship. This section will examine several human needs that require relationship to fulfill.

Humans Need Security

Humans have a desire for two types of security. First is a security in this life related to meeting basic physical and social needs. Second, we need to feel secure beyond this life.

Temporal Security

In the United States, the largest cause for breakups of marriage and relationships are financial difficulties. When people fail to properly manage their finances in a marriage relationship, life is difficult. In our society, money is at the center of almost all of our decisions. Since most of us don't live on farms, don't grow our own food, or raise our own livestock, we have to use money to purchase our food. Since many of us do not own our houses outright, we have mortgages and we have to make payments. Since most of us are not energy independent, we have to purchase electricity from a company. The list goes on and on. We even give to our churches by writing checks, making direct deposits, or placing cash in a collection plate. Money is all around us. We deal with it, day in and day out.

It's no wonder that, when families struggle over money, it strains the marriage relationship. When a married couple is unable to have financial security, the frustration will often bleed over into other areas. When people don't feel secure, they can become agitated easily. Lack of security and personal finance can poison a relationship. On the other hand, when families are financially secure, they tend to be more at ease. Mistakes that individuals make have a more realistic presentation, when the family is confident in their situation. A well-stocked pantry and a comfortable emergency fund go a long way to providing harmony in a family.

When we have certain basic needs met, we can focus on other things that we find more desirable and perhaps more important in the long run. Security not only in finances and food but in relation to safety and the predictability of our lives help us to feel more alive, more in control.

Throughout our history, families have been the basic unit for providing security and stability. In the ancient world, the patriarch of the family was responsible for provision and cohesion within the family group. The matriarch also directed and supported the family. In a chaotic and sometimes dangerous world, the family was a unit of stability, refuge, and strength.

Beyond the family, clans, and eventually nations and states became the basis of security. Ultimately for Christians, a relationship with God is a major factor in temporal security. Depending on others in relationship is a way to meet the needs that humans have for security in this life. Whether it is for finances, food, or safety, relationship is the primary means of establishing security.

Transcendent Security

Beyond being secure in the day-to-day workings of life, humans also wonder about what lies beyond death. The concept of existence beyond physical death is pervasive throughout human history. Humans have struggled with the finiteness of life throughout all of civilization. Each culture had some conception of existence or meaning beyond the end of physical life.

In Christianity, the conception of the afterlife has been tied to the ultimate purpose of the creation of human beings. Christians are reassured by the promises they find in the Bible and the promises from the lips of Jesus that their life after death will be meaningful and secure.

Humans Need Love

While it's not true that all you need is love, we certainly do need it. Humans need both to love and to be loved. Humans are emotional creatures; we feel deeply. Although love is more than a feeling, it certainly has an emotional feeling attached to it. Clifford Williams claims that we want to be loved by our parents, friends, and later by a spouse. In addition, he claims that we want to deeply care about others, to know them and trust them.[2]

If Williams is correct, then love relationships are important and indeed needed by humans. That is to say, humans need to experience love both as the recipient and as the giver. It is not enough to be loved in isolation.

---

2. Williams, *Existential Reasons for Belief*, 24–25.

Neither is it enough to love in isolation. Only through a reciprocal loving relationship (or relationships) is the human need for love met.

Humans can meet this need for love within many types of relationships. Humans can love other nonhuman creatures. Many people have pets to which they show and receive affection. On television and on the Internet, you can see testimonial after testimonial from pet lovers. People take their companions with them wherever they go. Humans can certainly have relationships to animals, and they can express affection and love to an animal. The animals can also return behaviors that humans interpret as loving. This is not the place to discuss whether or not animals can love, especially the way that humans can love, but certainly some people find great comfort in relationships with animals.

Humans can also have the need for love met within other human relationships. Williams is right to note that the first loving relationship that many people have is with a parent or caregiver. Parents bond with their children and the children come to love their parents, biological or not. Children have a desire to be loved by their parents. Indeed, many self-destructive behaviors can manifest when that desire is not met. Parental love is a type of relationship where the child can reciprocate. Parents can express love to their children, and their children can express love back. In fact, that's the way it should be.

Another type of human relationship where the need for love can be met is within the sibling relationship. Brothers and sisters can have a special love for one another that is related to being part of the same family. Spending significant time with one another when young can provide bonding experiences and connections that last a lifetime. In the ancient cultures that produced the Bible, the sibling relationship took greater priority than the marital relationship. Blood was thicker than marriage. Brothers and sisters valued one another because of their family connections.

A third type of human relationship where the need for love can be met is within friendships. Because of shared circumstances or prolonged time together in a way that is similar to a sibling relationship, people can love one another through their friendships. Friendships can develop in any number of ways and can be fostered with any number of experiences. The acceptance and love that comes from close friendships is important and can be very strong.

A fourth type of human relationship with the need for love can be met within a sexual relationship. Normally, and normatively for Christians, this relationship should be the marriage relationship. Ideally a marriage relationship would include all of the benefits of a friendship as well as the intimacy of a sexual relationship.

Humans have the ability to satisfy their need for love and relationships with animals, other humans, and also with God. God created humans for fellowship with himself. He is love and has shown that to humanity in innumerable ways. From creating, providing, directing, chastising, and redeeming, God has demonstrated his love toward humanity. God also invites humans to express and demonstrate their love to him. God has provided internal and external acts of devotion as ways for humans to reciprocate their love for him. God has provided a way for humans to be loved by him and to express their love to him in relationship with himself.

Humans Need Acceptance

> As for wise counsel, a warm hug, or a swift kick in the rear, those are rather hard to self-administer. If we don't already have those kinds of relationships in place, it's usually too late to pull them together once a need to know or need to grow crisis hits with full force.[3]

Closely related to love is acceptance. Our strong drive for autonomy and individuality makes us take a risk that we might not be accepted by others. We have, however, a need to be accepted by others. Belonging to a group may help meet our need for security, but it also contributes to our need to be accepted. Joining with a group for protection is fine, but we also want to feel like we belong because of common traits or interests. The only way that we can truly be part of a group, a voluntary group, is to attempt to join it and risk rejection.

As humans, we want to tell others who we are; it is part of our autonomous need. And we also want others to accept us when we tell them who we are. That is our need to be accepted into a group. Being part of a group allows individuals to share experiences and stories. It allows for understanding and affirmation. In some ways, acceptance is closely tied to being understood. Perhaps we actually have a need to feel like we are rational, like we have made good decisions in the choices we made. Not simply that we did make choices, but that they were justified.

---

3. Osborn, *Sticky Church*, 58.

Becoming part of a community that accepts us "as we are" is a legitimate human need. To say that we desire to be accepted, however, does not mean that we should not desire change. We should not forget that acceptance is not identical to approval. While we may seek approval on certain things, seeking to belong and be accepted for who we are is not the same as wanting approval for our choices and actions. An individual may choose to become part of a group who accepts others based on their failures rather than on accomplishments. Many twelve-step programs require individuals to admit that they had a problem with addiction as part of acceptance into the group; however, the goal is not to stay that way, but to improve or overcome. It is important that we not confuse acceptance with approval. Humans generally have a need for acceptance, and may desire approval, but they are not the same.

Humans Need Affirmation

In a way that is similar to a need for acceptance, humans also have a need to be affirmed. Humans desire affirmation. In life we have to make an innumerable number of choices. Some of these choices have to be made with little to no information. When things don't go the way that we hoped, we experience regret and sorrow. Humans long for someone to come alongside us and tell us that we did the best we could. We make mistakes and we need to hear about them. We also need people to realize that when we did the best we could, even if things turned out poorly, others understand. We need to know that they affirm the direction that we took.

As we order our lives and plan the tasks and objectives that we find important, we want others to come alongside and support or affirm us. Affirmation is similar to acceptance, but it is not entirely the same. Affirmation may come from a member of a group that we are associated with, or from someone else. Affirmation may take the form of compensation for a job well done.

Humans Need Connection to Be Understood

Humans have a desire to connect with others. We also have a desire to be understood. Being understood does not necessarily mean affirmed or accepted, but it can. Since we are unique from the rest of creation, we desire a connection with someone who understands what we are like. This type of need usually includes a reciprocal aspect. We need someone else who we can know and understand as well.

The ability to be known and to know another can provide deep connections for humans. A friend who understands you and whom you understand can provide a great sense of comfort and satisfaction. The ability to anticipate someone's needs and the assurance that comes from the expectation that another person is able to anticipate your needs is the essence of connectedness and understanding.

When humans have experiences that are extraordinarily stressful or exhilarating, having someone who can anticipate them provides deep satisfaction. When my wife comes home after a particularly difficult day and I'm able to anticipate what she will need to improve her mood or make her feel better, I gain a sense of value to her. In addition, she senses her value to me, and the fact that I know her intimately enough to be able to meet the need or desire that she has without her having to express it.

This type of intimacy and connection may represent the inter-Trinitarian relationships that God experiences. The relationship does not necessarily have to be a marital relationship, some friendships may extend to this kind of understanding and connection. Often, however, marital relationships do find a connection that is very close and intimate.

Humans Need Justice and Order

Since God is orderly and not chaotic, it makes sense that humans would have a desire for order rather than chaos. Humans have needs for stability in relational matters, as well as in the ordering of the world.

Equity and Fairness

Something disturbs humans when things seem unfair. You don't have to teach a child to demand justice when they feel like they are being wronged; they just do it. Very few day-care centers or households with young children have failed to hear the cries of young ones demanding justice. If someone refuses to share, or someone takes something that belongs to another, children are quick to demand justice and equity.

When people are successful, we want to believe that they worked hard and they deserved what they got. When we see someone getting something they did not deserve, we hope that the tables will be turned and things will be set right. We want what we think we deserve and we don't like it when we receive something we do not feel that we deserved. We have a desire for justice and order. We don't like when things go differently than we think they should.

The call for justice is reasonable and expected given that we are created in God's image, we know about God and his requirements for our lives, and we have his laws written in our hearts. Because humanity has an innate understanding of God and his attributes, it is not unreasonable to assume that humans desire justice and order. After all, justice and order are both attributes of God (see Romans 1 and 2).

Christianity satisfies the human need for order and justice. The Christian concept of a sovereign God directing and ordering his creation to just end allows us to anticipate final justice. Ultimately the wrongs of the world will be set right by God, who knows and sees all.

Stability with Variety in the World

Humans like things to remain stable, but they also like variation. Humans are creatures of habit—we like to eat the same kinds of food over and over again. We like to go to the same places repeatedly. When we gather in church, we tend to sit in the same area or with the same people over and over. But we do not like everything to be exactly the same. Although we have certain foods that we like, we do eat a wide variety. Some of this may be related to nutritional needs, but part of it is simply personal preference. Although we like routine, we also like variation.

Beyond meeting simple needs, like eating, we also like the world to be predictable in the way it functions. Imagine if the world was the kind of place where you might drop something one day and it falls to the ground. The next day you drop the same thing and it rises in the sky. That kind of world would be very difficult to live in. We need order in the world. Although we like the natural world to function in a regular way, we get bored. Many people long for the seasons to change because of the variety of weather that comes with it.

God has ordered the world in such a way that there is a tremendous amount of stability and there's also a stimulating amount of variety. Humans order our lives around the two-pronged fork of stability and variety. Our world also has natural consequences for actions. If you drop an egg, not only will it fall, it will also break when it hits the ground. If you drop an egg tomorrow, it will do the same thing. The consequences that come from taking certain actions are regular and predictable. Whether these are described as natural or anticipated consequences, the point is that human life is based around an understanding of consequences for actions.

Since we experience a world with a large degree of consistency in consequences, we can function. We can manipulate the world around us. Our ability to manipulate the world and anticipate consequences of our actions gives us endless variety. This world is designed for humans to experience stability and predictability with variation. This world is designed to allow humans to meet their needs.

Chapter Four

God's Relationship to Humanity

AS CREATOR

THE FIRST AND MOST basic way that people relate to God is as creature to Creator. Everything in creation, other than God, is dependent on God. The creation itself would not exist if not for God. This section will examine how God relates to humans as both transcendent Creator and immanent Creator.

The creation has a natural order, which ancient societies commonly understood. In the Christian view, we find that the creation is ordered in the following manner. God, who is the Creator, stands preeminent, above the created order. Heavenly beings are the next rank. The heavenly beings have tasks to perform for God within the heavenly realm. Humans find themselves next in the ordering of creation and part of the physical realm. Humans also have tasks to perform for God in the physical realm. After humans in prominence are animals, followed by plants, and finally inanimate objects.

Within this order, humans are placed in the physical realm, but humans are not completely physical creatures. Unlike animals, plants, and inanimate objects, part of the human constitution is transcendent and spiritual. The physical world allows humans to reflect both aspects of our

God's Relationship to Humanity

nature. We are bound to, and part of, the physical world. We also transcend the physical world, to a degree, and exert authority over it.

Transcendent

> Within the cosmos we are the restless creatures that look beyond the material universe for ultimate fulfillment. We are designed to find our meaning and identity in relation to, and only in relation to, God.[1]

God is beyond the creation. God is before the creation. All that is created belongs to him and exists because of his good pleasure. Humans are physical creatures with a divine image that connects us to the transcendent Creator. God has created humans with the ability to transcend their physical world and to use that transcendence to exercise dominion over it.

Our transcendent relationship to God is based on the creature to Creator relationship and the *imago dei*. God, who transcends the entire creation, shares with humanity the ability to shape the world. Through human rationality and will, we can respond to the physical world in ways that the lower ranking creatures cannot. Stanley Grenz writes, "as humans we enjoy the possibility of transcending any finite ordering of our environment . . . This is linked to our ability of self-transcendence, which makes us unique from the animals"[2]

The image of God makes us able to shape the physical world to our liking. It also pushes us to be more than what we are. Because our transcendence makes us like God, and unlike the rest of the creation, we yearn to comprehend more. We examine the boundaries of our existence and question them, exploring the physical world and the world of our thought and imagination. We seek to be like our Creator by creating. From architecture to art, humans use their thoughts and imagination to bring into existence things that did not exist. We shape wood, stone, metal, and plastic into beautiful carvings, structures, and tools.

Our touching of the spiritual plane of existence makes us yearn for more than we can find in the physical realm. God relates to humanity as the Creator that is beyond the creation. We understand this, to some degree, because we also transcend the creation. Rather than simply relating to God

---

1. Grenz, *Community of God*, 132.
2. Grenz, *Community of God*, 131.

as a creature that is wholly different than he, we relate to him as creatures who have a reverberation of his spirit within our own.

The ape, the lion, and the locust can never understand the transcendence of God, since they cannot have the experience of transcending their own states. They are able to find complete contentment in their physical existence because they are physical, and that is the totality of what they are.

We enter into relationship with our Creator as one who has transcendence, albeit limited, over his own world. We have the ability to transcend because the transcendent Creator gave it to us so that we could be in relationship with him. Our ability to understand God's transcendent nature is derivative of our own ability to experience transcendence.

Although God shares with humanity the ability to transcend the physical world, we should not forget that God's transcendence is far beyond our own. Every attribute shared by God with his creation is possessed by the creature to a degree much less than the way God himself possesses it. Therefore, it is not in an attitude of arrogance that we emphasize our likeness to God, but in gratitude. Our existence is dependent on him, as are our attributes. We should praise God and rejoice in that which he has given to us. Seeking to minimize or downplay humanity is not an act of humility, but one that diminishes God's glory in his creation and salvation of mankind.

Immanent

> "For in him we live and move and have our being." As some of your own poets have said, "We are his offspring." (Acts 17:28)

> This Human incapability to be fulfilled by any structure of the world, in turn, drives us beyond the finitude of our experience in a never-ending quest for fulfillment. We are, therefore, dependent creatures. But our dependency is greater than the finite world can ever satisfy.[3]

While God exists beyond his creation, he is also present to his creation. God is not a distant observer having only muted experiences of the universe. God is close. He hears the crashing of the ocean waves. He feels the rustling of leaves in the forests and the cascading of the water along the rocks. He feels the heat and light of the stars. He feels the magnificent pull

---

3. Grenz, *Community of God*, 131.

of the black hole's gravity and observes the fuzzy darting back and forth of the electrons dancing with the protons of every atom. He sees the cosmic rays from their origin to their terminus. God also sees humans in all of our glory and folly, in all of our need and abundance, in all of our strength and weakness.

God knows us, our capabilities and limitations, better than we ever will. In all of our longing to be, God is alongside us. When we learn how to stand, walk, and run, he is there. When we start to ponder, he knows not only what we are thinking, but how and why we are thinking it. When we think we are alone and no one cares or understands, God is both caring and understanding of our experience of loneliness.

God has been present for everything we have ever experienced. While that might make us cringe, given some of our indiscretions, it means that God truly understands us. And although God is great and understands everything in the creation, he also understands everything about us. If transcendence is our way to connect to God, immanence is God's way to connect to us.

We relate to God as beings that exist within his creation. We respond to the physical processes of our bodies. Sometimes we respond well, and other times we do not. Our physical nature drives us to meet physical needs just as our transcendent nature drives us to meet transcendent needs. We work creation to provide sustenance and shelter. We seek physical companionship and long for the embrace of those we love. We are physical creatures in a physical world. While the totality of our existence is not physical, we should neither deny nor diminish our physicality. To be human, in part, involves being a physical being. God is glorified in our physical nature, just as he is glorified in our transcendent nature.

AS REDEEMER

Early in the human story, rebellion appears. Humans, who had been in a close relationship with God, attempt to become more than what God had created them to be. Eve and Adam seek to go beyond the boundaries God established. By taking from the Tree of The Knowledge of Good and Evil, they thought they would become more than they were. By partaking of the fruit, they came to know evil in a personal way, by committing sin. With the violation of God's command, the sin of rebellion entered into the human heart and has found fertile ground there ever since.

Shortly after expulsion from the garden, things get worse. Cain, while working the soil, allows sin to take root and brings in a harvest of murder. From there, evil in the heart of humanity springs forth like the weeds (thorns and thistles) spring forth from the soil to choke out the crops. As humanity expands, the evil committed expands as well.

God, being loving, provides a way for his people to reconcile with him. If God did not act, humans would not have any way to return from their rebellion. The sacrificial system of the Old Testament was the first way God provided for people to come back to him. The ultimate act of reconciliation, however, was the self-sacrifice of Jesus.

Sacrificial System

Sacrifices made to God are seen as soon as Genesis 4, as Cain and Abel are shown to bring offerings to God. Outside of the Bible, we know that sacrifice to deities are part of the landscape of ancient peoples. Pagans would make sacrifices of various kinds to manifold idols as tribute, petition, or for reconciliation, a common practice throughout human history.

The particular emphasis in the Old Testament sacrificial system for sin was surrounding the blood of the animal. Oblation of blood was used when making sacrifices for sins; it was seen as containing the creature's life, and therefore special. The blood was splashed against the altar for forgiveness of sins. Blood was treated as sacred because it represented life, which comes from and belongs to God. The respect for blood extends to dietary laws, as well.

> I will set my face against any Israelite or any foreigner residing among them who eats blood, and I will cut them off from the people. For the life of a creature is in the blood, and I have given it to you to make atonement for yourselves on the altar; it is the blood that makes atonement for one's life. Therefore I say to the Israelites, "None of you may eat blood, nor may any foreigner residing among you eat blood."
>
> Any Israelite or any foreigner residing among you who hunts any animal or bird that may be eaten must drain out the blood and cover it with earth, because the life of every creature is its blood. That is why I have said to the Israelites, "You must not eat the blood of any creature, because the life of every creature is its blood; anyone who eats it must be cut off." (Lev 17:10–14)

God's Relationship to Humanity

The blood of domestic and wild animals is treated with reverence because of God's commands.

Sacrifice of an animal for sin is a type of exchange. When a human commits a sin, they take something that belongs to God for themselves. If, for example, I take credit for an accomplishment without acknowledging God, I have robbed God of some of the glory due him. If I trespass the boundaries God has set forth, I assert my will above his and rob him of some of the glory due him. When I take what belongs to God, I owe him. I have an obligation to repay or satisfy my debt.

My life is the payment I have for my debt to God. Since he created everything and owns it all, I cannot repay my debt with physical things. Life is given by God and is valuable to him. When I am indebted to God, my life is the one thing of value that I have. The sacrificial system allowed the life of animals to substitute for the life of humans. When God commands Abraham to sacrifice Isaac, we see that God himself provides a ram as a substitute for Isaac. God accepts the life of the ram as a substitute for Isaac's life.

In the sacrificial system, God demands payment for human sin, but he has also provided the means of payment in the blood of animals. Animal life replaces human life to atone for the sins of the humans. In this process, the life of the creature of lesser value, the animal, is exchanged for the life of an image bearer of God, the human. God has no obligation to accept the inferior life for the life of the human but, in his graciousness, he does. God accepts the animal life, as if it were human, and the debt is settled. What an amazing and gracious act of God in allowing human atonement with animal life.

The sacrificial system works, but there is a problem, not with the sacrificial system or with the sacrifices, but with us. We keep sinning, even after we have repented and sacrificed. In the sacrificial system, humans were able to restore their relationship with God, much like paying a speeding ticket. When you pay a speeding ticket, you restore the relationship between you and the state. But paying the ticket does not mean you will not drive over the speed limit again and get another ticket. Humans might pay for their sin with animal sacrifice only to incur new debts to God for further sins.

The sacrificial system provides a transactional relationship with God. Our violation of God's prerogative indebted us to God. Animal sacrifice provided a way to wipe the slate clean. Human relationship with God was one of regular indebtedness followed by periods of settled accounts.

Eventually the solemn nature of the exchange was lost, and people began to provide offerings that were inadequate. The pedantic nature of the regulations and customs that grew up around the sacrificial system led some to shortcut the process or ignore it all together. While the system of exchanging animal life for human life to settle human debt to God was adequate, this type of process can lead to an external obedience and legalism void of the immensely personal exchange that takes place in the sacrifice.

The relationship of God to his people through the sacrificial system was one of constant exchange. Humans constantly incurred debt that needed repayment. The focus of such a relationship was avoidance of debt and speedy repayment when debt was incurred. Intimacy in this relationship was seen in the grace of God providing and accepting an alternative payment in exchange for human life. God was glorified in his grace and mercy toward humanity. Humans glorified God by seeking to restore their relationship to God through the means he provided. Sacrificial animals glorified God by exchanging their life for human life and being accepted by God for that purpose.

Jesus

The perfection of the sacrificial system was God's own sacrifice of himself to himself. If animal sacrifice is accepting an inferior sacrifice for human life, the sacrifice of Jesus is a superior sacrifice being made for human life. The efficacious act of Jesus to atone for all human sin is possible because his life was infinitely more valuable than the human life for which he atoned.

For Christians, Jesus' death on the cross is the ultimate sacrifice for human sin. Jesus did not die in the temple, like animal sacrifices did, because human sacrifice was not permitted by God. Humans have no right to offer the life of another human in place of their own. Temple worship was not designed to accommodate the type of sacrifice Jesus made.

Although the Romans crucified Jesus and the Jews condemned him, Jesus is the priest who makes the sacrifice to the Father. He laid down his life—no one took it from him. He submitted to the Father's will till the end. Jesus, being fully human but not merely human, was a superior sacrifice to animals. Since he was a sinless human, he had no sin of his own to repay, but he laid down his life. Since he is divine, his life was not equal to human life, but infinitely superior.

God's Relationship to Humanity

Unlike the animal sacrifice, where an inferior life is graciously allowed to substitute for human life, Jesus' sacrifice is infinitely more valuable. The efficaciousness of Jesus' sacrifice is unbounded because the value of his life was limitless. Human indebtedness to God can never exceed the account of value coming from Jesus' sacrificial death.

If we were to look at the differential in exchange in terms of coins, humans might be silver and incur debts in the same terms. God was gracious to accept payment in the form of animal sacrifice. Animals might be thought of in terms of copper. Animal sacrifice paid debts due in the form of a silver coin with a copper coin. The copper was inherently less valuable, but God graciously accepted payment of a copper coin for a debt of a silver one. Jesus' life might be thought of in terms of gold. Humans still incur a debt of a silver coin, but payment is now rendered as a gold coin. The gold is inherently more valuable than the silver.

Unlike the animal sacrifice, the grace coming from God in Jesus' sacrifice is not the unequal exchange, but the payment itself. Although God graciously provided animals to be sacrificed, by creating them and allowing them to procreate, humans had to raise or purchase the animals and bring them to the temple for sacrifice. Humans have to initiate the sacrificial process to atone for their sin. God took all of the initiative in the case of Jesus.

The relationship of God to his people through the sacrifice of Jesus is one of excessive grace. Humans constantly incur debt to God, and that has already been paid. The focus of such a relationship is gratitude. Intimacy is seen by God providing an all-sufficient atonement for human sin and by humans relying on God's provision. God is glorified in his grace and mercy to humanity. Humans glorify God by their relationship to God and by emulating Jesus.

> Animal Sacrifice: Grace comes in God accepting an inferior sacrifice for human life.
>
> Christ's Sacrifice: Grace comes in God providing the sacrifice.

AS COMFORTER

Beyond a transactional relationship with God, humans also have an intimacy with God through his special care for his people. When Jesus was getting ready for the crucifixion, he told his disciples that he would send the Holy Spirit. Jesus said that it was good for him to go away so that the Spirit could come to his followers. The coming of the Holy Spirit universalized Jesus' ministry and empowered the church. The Holy Spirit both indwells believers and acts as an advocate on our behalf.

Indwelling Spirit

> If you love me, keep my commands. And I will ask the Father, and he will give you another advocate to help you and be with you forever—the Spirit of truth. The world cannot accept him, because it neither sees him nor knows him. But you know him, for he lives with you and will be in you. (John 14:15-17)

The concept that the Spirit of God lives inside of Christians is amazing. Humans have always had an issue of separation from their deities. For the Greeks, the gods lived high on Olympus. For the Egyptians, some of the gods were far off, like Ra the sun god and Nut the sky goddess. People might have prayed to them, but the gods were far away from the people. Worshipers might take offerings and sacrifices to temples, but the gods themselves lived far away.

The Holy Spirit is not far from Christians—in fact, he lives within them. The body of the believer becomes the temple for God's Spirit. The interesting aspect of this is the reversal of the typical pattern in religious life. Throughout history, humans sought ways to approach the divine. Through pilgrimage, people attempted to go to the place where God was. Through meditation, people sought to see through the illusion of the world and catch a glimpse of the deity surrounding them. Travel to sacred places; mystical rituals, rites, or experiences; and the use of substances to alter consciousness have been used to help humans connect to the transcendent.

Humans have sought ways to go beyond the physical so they could touch the face of God. Even in the Old Testament we see Moses on the mountain with God and the Israelites following his presence in the wilderness. Things change, however, after Jesus sends the Holy Spirit to be with his people. Now, instead of humans taking initiative to search for God, God comes closer to humans than they could ever have come to him. By taking residence in our own bodies, as a temple, Christians do not have to go on a pilgrimage to seek God. He is already with them. Jesus' people do not have to try to coax the divine down from some solitary mountain or across some other dimension so that they can commune together, since God dwells in their being.

With the sending of the Holy Spirit and the universalizing of Jesus' ministry, the issue of humans seeking God's presence has been solved by God residing in them. God is able to relate to Christians from within our very being. That is not to say that God possesses us. The concept of the Holy Spirit indwelling a believer is unlike demon possession. The indwelling of the Holy Spirit is about God being close and intimate with his people, while possession is about domination and control. The Holy Spirit does not dominate the humans and control them, though we sometimes pray that he would control us so that we would do better.

Because of the indwelling of the Holy Spirit, God relates to his people and is available to his people always. If we need to share a fear, need, concern, or anything else with God, we have no barrier to prevent us from sharing those things. We don't have to go to a sacred grove, temple, or even an altar. We have access to God regardless of where we are, whether we are sitting, standing, or laying down. Nothing about our location or circumstances prevents us from being in God's presence, since he is present to our being and will always be present to us.

Advocate on our Behalf

> In the same way, the Spirit helps us in our weakness. We do not know what we ought to pray for, but the Spirit himself intercedes for us through wordless groans. And he who searches our hearts knows the mind of the Spirit, because the Spirit intercedes for God's people in accordance with the will of God. (Rom 8:26–27)

Humans are in rebellion against God. We have robbed God of his glory and taken liberties for ourselves that belong to him alone. Historically people have made sacrifices or taken part in rituals to attempt to atone for their transgressions, and the Bible makes the point of human culpability before God very clear. Christianity, once again, changes the paradigm when it comes to people pleading their own position to God. God the Holy Spirit advocates for believers.

It is not uncommon for a religion to have priests. A priest is one who will intercede with the deity for the benefit of the people. Indeed, the Old Testament sets up the sacrificial system and God appointed priests to fulfill the role of intercession. The New Testament tells us that Jesus fulfills the role of the high priest and intercedes for us. The Holy Spirit also intercedes for us. We have advocates before the Father on our behalf. These advocates are perfect because they are themselves divine.

When we do not know what to pray or how to pray, we can find confidence that God knows our situation and is even advocating for our position. Jesus and the Holy Spirit are interceding for us, even when we don't have any idea of how to plead our case. The need to represent ourselves before God is eliminated because God himself represents us.

We can relate to God knowing he is concerned with our good. Part of the special relationship with God is grounded in the fact that we don't have to be concerned about God tricking us or taking advantage of us. Because God advocates for us, he views us through the lens of seeking what is best for us. We need to remember that what is actually best for us may not be what we think is best. Sometimes we need a reality check. Sometimes the loving thing to do is to let us fail. Sometimes a painful experience brings about more good in the long term than avoiding the painful experience would. Because God is our advocate, we can have confidence that he is bringing us into circumstances that will ultimately be for our benefit.

AS FATHER

When examining some of the ways that God relates to his people, it might be thought that the Father is against humanity and the Son and the Spirit are for humanity. While it is true that Jesus and the Holy Spirit have played special roles in the redemption of humanity, the Father is the one who sent them and they are fulfilling his plan. God the Father is not a vengeful deity on a cloud waiting to smite someone. He is a loving and caring God who seeks to have humanity function for its own good and be in a loving relationship with him.

We will examine three aspects of this loving intervention by the Father for humanity. We will find that God relates to humanity as Father in these three ways. First, through adoption, God makes humans part of his family. Second, by providing for our needs, God shows his love to us. Third, by guiding us, God shows his loving interest and care for us.

Adoption

Adoption is a doctrine not often discussed. We like to talk about being in God's family. Sometimes people speak about the church being God's family.

In discussions of salvation, however, this concept can be overlooked. Often Christians speak of salvation in forensic, or legal terms. That is not wrong, but it is not the entire story.

When people become Christians, God adopts us into his family. The concept of adoption is important, because family is important. The first institution we find in the Bible is the creation of the family with the establishment of marriage. With family comes responsibility and privilege. Responsibility to seek the good of the family is inherent in the institution. The patriarch has the ultimate responsibility to his family and should provide and protect them. Other members of the family also share in this responsibility, but historically this duty fell to the patriarch. Heirs would sleep under the protection and provision of the patriarch and would seek to shoulder a portion of that responsibility, as they were able.

Being part of a family brought not just responsibility, but also privilege. The provision of the family was shared within the family. The flocks and fields had to be worked, of course, but the harvest was also shared. When the family had blessings, those blessings would be shared. When time came for the inheritance to be distributed, it was the family who received it. Sons and daughters would receive special blessing from their family that was not given to outsiders.

Because we are adopted into God's family, we relate to God as children and heirs. The status we share means we have responsibility, yes, but it also means we share in the blessings. We expect that God will provide for us and give us good things because we are his. God may bless those who are outside of his family, but as insiders, we expect very good things from our Father.

Adoption allows humans to relate to God, and not just as creature to Creator. Christians have the privilege to relate to God as an heir relates to a good father. A good father wants to bless his children and seeks to ensure that they have good things. As discussed previously, we should not confuse good things with eliminating or withholding painful or difficult experiences. Sometimes a loving act is not necessarily pleasant.

Provision

We often talk about God meeting our needs. Sometimes this talk is focused on material needs, which God does meet. But our needs are beyond just the material. God provides for all of his creation, but he provides for his people in ways that the rest of the creation does not get to experience.

We get good things from God and because we are part of his family we expect that he will give us good things. James confirms our understanding that the Father is the source of the good things we have. "Every good and perfect gift is from above, coming down from the Father of the heavenly lights, who does not change like shifting shadows" (Jas 1:17). When we have the food we need, we understand that God has provided it for our benefit. Sometimes that provision is supernatural, but most often God provides food for the world by having people work the ground. Going back to Adam, the way that people eat is from working of the land.

Although most of God's provision for humanity comes through means that require effort on our part, sometimes his provision is unexpected, or at least not directly brought about through human planning. Sometimes volunteer crops grow in fields that have not been worked. Other times people simply harvest what they need from the land around them. The wilderness provides plants and animals for human sustenance.

In addition to intentional human agricultural production and harvesting from land that has not been cultivated, God has also provided for his people in miraculous ways. The Bible recounts a number of times when God provided for his people in a more direct fashion. From the wilderness wanderings when God provided manna, quail, and water, to the abundance of oil from a small jar, God has sometimes provided miraculously. Jesus provided large catches of fish for his disciples and fed multitudes as signs of who he was. God can and has provided for his people in miraculous ways.

God provides more than just food. God gives us the means to provide shelter and clothing. In the modern world, he gives us the ability to earn money to provide the things we need. God's provision extends beyond physical needs to our emotional and spiritual needs. As social creatures, we need to have relationships. We can have a relationship with God, but we also need to have relationships with other humans.

Communities and families allow us to have relationships with others that provide fulfillment and stimulation. God provides people for us to have relationships with and will also move people in and out of our lives for our own good. God provides the different types of relationships we need to mature and develop. Sometimes we have to search for those relationships, so we should not exclude the idea that we have to participate in the process.

In fact, sometimes searching for a specific relationship allows us to learn things that we might have missed if we did not have to search for it.

God also provides a way for us to have our spiritual needs met. We are in rebellion against God until we are reconciled with him through Jesus. God did not leave us in our pitiful state without providing a solution. Prior to Jesus' first advent, the sacrificial system of the Old Testament served as a way to reconcile with the God we rebelled against. God has provided ways for our spiritual needs to be met.

We relate to God as provider because he has provided for us and continues to do so. We are confident in God's provision because it is all that has sustained us or ever will sustain us. Even in the state of rebellion, God gave us good things because he loves us. God has the sun shine on the good and the evil, he sends rain to the just and unjust (Matt 5:45).

Guidance

God meets our needs, and as children we expect good things from him. He also tells us what we should do. We often ask for God to guide us as we pray. God guides us toward what is good. The ways God can guide us are varied. We will examine five ways that God guides his people.

First, God guides his people through Scripture. The concept that God uses his revealed word to guide his people should not be a difficult one. Part of the purpose of Scripture is to provide instruction for his people. Although the purpose of Scripture is more than simply providing guidance to God's people, we should readily accept that providing guidance is one part of the purpose.

Second, God guides his people through prayer. If prayer is talking to God, then it should not be surprising that, in our conversations with God, he guides us. Whether the guidance comes from an external response from God or from a realization of his will through the forming of our petitions, it is there nonetheless. Praying alone or with others allows God to provide guidance to his people.

Third, God guides his people through others. Sometimes these people are also believers, and sometimes they are not. The people we interact with on a daily basis and those who only occasionally come into our lives are used by God to provide guidance. Our family and fellow believers are there to help us talk through situations and figure out what God is leading us to do. Biological family and church family both have a vested interest in our guidance based on their relationship to us. To the degree that we have more people in our lives who are themselves Christians, we can expect God to provide more and more guidance through them. We should not forget, however, that God can and does use unbelievers to guide us. Sometimes guidance is negative (a scary person waiting in a dark alley might encourage us not to enter), but sometimes guidance is positive (helping someone or being helped may start a relationship or provide information).

Fourth, God guides his people through their circumstances. God may place you in circumstances that provide only one option. If he does that, the choice is clear. Most of the time, however, we have multiple options and need to determine which one to take. Simply examining our situation might make the guidance clear as God is rational and often provides us with good reasons for choosing the things we do.

Fifth, God guides his people by direct intervention. God might directly intervene in a situation by removing or placing an obstacle. In Exodus, he placed a pillar of fire to block the Egyptians while parting the sea for the Israelites. He may override our will and cause us to do something we did not intend. We may be unable to identify when God directly intervenes for any number of reasons. God's intervention might be beyond our ability to perceive, and it may have been in the past before we ever knew there would be an issue.

We relate to God as a trusted guide in matters that trouble us or cause us concern. The more we realize that God guides us in various ways, the more we are able to trust him when the guidance takes us into difficult places.

AS FRIEND

Although we have examined some ways humans are able to relate to God, we have one final category to explore: that of friend. Friendship with God is a type of relationship lacking from most other religious systems. For someone to have a friendship with another, the other must themselves be a person. Deity as a person is missing in pantheistic religions. Pagan religions picture the gods as having friendships, but often those relationship are among other deities, not with humans. In Islam, the radical transcendence of Allah makes it difficult to see how humans could be a friend.

Christianity (and to some extent Judaism) presents God as one that can have humans as a friend. The Old Testament gives us examples of people relating to God in ways reminiscent of friendship. The New Testament affirms some of the Old Testament examples, and Jesus calls his followers his friends.

Direct to God (External)

God sought to be in relationship with humans from the garden onward. Genesis tells us that God walked in the garden, and it seems that Adam and Eve may have been accustomed to spending time with God prior to the fall. After the fall, however, they wanted to hide from God because they felt shame.

Even Cain is shown to have a relationship to God where he receives advice and is in God's presence. God tells Cain that he should not let sin rule over him. However, Cain does not heed that advice and kills his brother. Even in the banishment of Cain, God protects his life by marking him.

Enoch is another person we see who has a special relationship with God. While there is not much said about Enoch in Genesis, we are told that he walked with God faithfully. The faithful relationship may be the reason that we are told that God took Enoch away. He simply was no more, meaning he was no longer in the land where his family was, but that God had taken him somewhere else.

Abraham is shown to have a close relationship with God, as well. God interacts and meets with Abraham on a number of occasions. He tests Abraham and blesses him. In the New Testament, James claims that Abraham was God's friend.

The New Testament also shows humans being God's friends. Jesus notes this in John's Gospel. He tells his disciples that they are not simply servants, but friends, because they know his will. The relationship has changed from one of mere obligation to one of love and respect.

Direct to God (Internal)

Through the ministry of the Holy Spirit, we are able to relate to God in intimate ways at all times. The ability to have immediate access to God at whenever we want makes true intimacy with God a possibility. No longer do we have to wait for God to arrive or hope that he can hear us. We have no physical barriers to keep us from God.

In Dominion

Sometimes friendships develop through shared experiences. Through work or hobbies, we may connect with others who have similar interests. Interests serve as the basis on which many friendships begin. Often, we will make friends with people we work or play with because we have some initial connections that allow the relationship to take root and grow.

God has called humans to exercise dominion over his creation. In exercising dominion, part of our transcendent nature is used to shape the physical world. God's dominion is far greater than ours, but we do share the ability to exercise it with him. We can connect to God in many ways, and this is one of those ways.

As we work the soil or animals, we find that our work demands that we give of ourselves to accomplish the task. Our blood, sweat, and tears go into the various vocations, especially those in agriculture. In exercising dominion, we learn to give of ourselves for the benefit of the animals or crops. We also have to schedule, manage, monitor, and plan our actions. Animals don't experience this kind of complex interrelatedness, but God does.

We can connect to God and develop a friendship with him in part because we understand how to give of ourselves. God gives of himself for his creation, and especially for us. We have an ability to experience giving of ourselves because of God giving us the task of exercising dominion on his behalf.

In Human Relationships

Human relationships are not only important for us, but they are most of what we know. Our rearing as children provides us with the first of the human relationships we will have. For many, this is a parent-to-child relationship. Family relationships are also some of the first and most formative relationships that we experience. As we continue to grow, we experience even more relationships outside of our families and in our various communities.

Because of the indwelling of the Holy Spirit in believers, the relationships with other humans allow us to encounter God in their lives. When two Christians spend time together and are friends, their friendship brings them closer not only to one another, but closer to God.

In Christian theology, the process of sanctification makes believers more like Jesus Christ. The more that a person becomes like Jesus through sanctification, the more they communicate God's character. In befriending a Christian, people have the ability to be close to someone who is modeling God's character. But the modeling of God's character is not mere imitation—it is an actual transformation being wrought by the Holy Spirit.

Humans have the ability to relate to God in our human relationships. All humans are created in God's image. On a basic level, human interaction is between image bearers of God. Relationship with a Christian provides an opportunity to relate to someone who is indwelt by God's Spirit. Relationships between Christians allow for interaction with people who are becoming progressively more sanctified. In the next chapter, we will examine the implications of relating to God through his people.

Chapter Five

God's People

GOD'S FAMILY

THE BIBLE USES FAMILY imagery to describe the relationship of God to his people. God is described as Father, and Jesus is God's Son. Christians are identified as siblings, brothers and sisters. It is not surprising that family imagery is used to describe the relationship between God and his people, as family is the basic unit of society.

Families were close-knit communities in the ancient Mediterranean world. The view of family in the United States and in Western societies is very different than the way families were viewed in biblical times. Loyalty to family was one of the most important aspects of the ancient family structure. The blood relationship between siblings was more important, and often more valued, than the marital relationship. Although this sounds odd to Western ears, the ancient world is filled with examples of siblings siding with one another over and against spouses.

Families sought to improve their status and protected themselves. Actions taken by members of a family were judged in relation to how the larger family benefited, and the focus was not on the personal satisfaction of an individual member. In other words, each individual had a responsibility to the family first. If their individual desires or ambitions conflicted with the needs of the family, they were expected to submit their desires for the greater good of the family.

When we are talking about being part of God's family, we should remember that tremendous responsibility comes to us. We have loyalty to God, as Father, but also to our siblings. When the early church called one another brothers and sisters, it was filled with the concept of being loyal to one another. While this project is not one to examine the social structure of the ancient family, we need to have a basic conception of the way those families functioned if we are to understand the significance of being in God's family. In Joseph Hellerman's work *When the Church Was a Family*, he does an excellent job of explaining the significance of family imagery and the relational expectations in the ancient world. He writes, "It is clear that the early Christians used 'brother' as the key image for community in the church and thereby drew the whole constellation of behavioral expectations and values associated with sibling relationships as they currently functioned in the patrilineal kinship groups of Mediterranean antiquity."[1] For the early church, the imagery of the family was not one of social politeness, but of deep commitment and value.

ADOPTION: JOINING THE FAMILY

Joining a family is not something we might think about very often. We may have daydreamed about being born into a wealthy family, a royal family, or even a very powerful family, because we like the idea of having the perks. Most of the time, we simply know that we are part of our family. Whether our family is healthy or abusive, has a good reputation or not, or helps or hinders our advancement is secondary, because we have little say into which family we belong. We are born into families and are stuck wherever we land. Adoption, however, provides an alternative means of joining a family.

As we have already mentioned, God adopts us into his family. When we are adopted, God becomes our Father, and we relate to him as such. But that is not all. Jesus, although divine, is also God's Son. The sonship of Christ is not only a sign of who Jesus is, but it places him in a priority position in the ordering of the siblings of the family. Adoption makes us not only God's children, but also siblings, by adoption, of Christ. When the Bible describes Christians as heirs and joint-heirs with Christ in Romans 8, it affirms the adoptive status we receive as believers. We have God as our

---

1. Hellerman, *Family*, 41.

Father and Christ as our brother, and we also get one another as brothers and sisters.

The realization that the church should relate to one another as siblings may not have sunk in yet. We may have little problem referring to one another as brother or sister on Sunday mornings, but when we start to realize the importance of the sibling bond in the ancient family, we will soon realize that our connections within the church are probably too superficial. Loving the church family takes on a new dimension when we realize that every believer has a special relationship to us. The church should not only view itself as a family, but it should function more like one. When Jesus told his disciples that they should have a special affection for one another, they understood that they should love one another like they loved their siblings.

Sanctification: Becoming More Like the Family

Joining the family is important because that is how you gain the church as family. But we cannot remain the same as we were before when we join our new family group. We have to learn how to be a part of the family. We have to learn the family's language, history, traditions, stories, and many other things. We learn these things in a way similar to the way children are introduced to their own families. If you were raised in a typical family, you learned how to get along with your parents, siblings, grandparents, aunts and uncles, and cousins. Becoming part of the church family, learning how to be a part of that family, and learning how to represent them is part of the growth process for a new Christian.

Young children are important, and are protected and provided for while they are young and immature. The family needs them to grow up and become a productive member if the family is going to prosper. As children mature, they take on responsibility and contribute to the good of the family. The church should be no different.

Christians need to understand their new status before God and within the worshiping community of the church. We call the process of becoming more Christlike "sanctification." Learning how to function within the church is important for the new believer. Learning the stories and teachings of the church are also important. This is crucial (and not just for new believers' growth) because believers will have the responsibility to teach new family members as well. As new believers incorporate Christian identity into themselves, they become a more productive and valuable member of the family. As we learn about the type of person we should be, and as we work to become more like the person we should be, we actually become more like the person we should be.

The sanctification process is gradual and communal. We do not grow in Christlike-ness through isolation, but in the process of being the church family. I know I might cause a stir with what I am going to write next, but it is much more important for us to do things together as a family, than to do them apart. In other words, it is more important for us to pray together than to pray alone. It is more important for us to read Scripture together than to read Scripture alone. Far too much focus has been placed on individual piety, and too little emphasis has been placed on practicing spiritual disciplines within the context of the church.

Someone might claim that Jesus would go out alone to pray. I agree. I am not saying that we should do everything as a family all the time. That would be impossible. But in the Gospels, Jesus is much more often seen with his disciples than alone. Even in Gethsemane, Jesus brought his disciples with him when he prayed in this difficult hour.

> Then Jesus went with his disciples to a place called Gethsemane, and he said to them, "Sit here while I go over there and pray." He took Peter and the two sons of Zebedee along with him, and he began to be sorrowful and troubled. Then he said to them, "My soul is overwhelmed with sorrow to the point of death. Stay here and keep watch with me." Going a little farther, he fell with his face to the ground and prayed, "My Father, if it is possible, may this cup be taken from me. Yet not as I will, but as you will." Then he returned to his disciples and found them sleeping. "Couldn't you men keep watch with me for one hour?" he asked Peter. "Watch and pray so that you will not fall into temptation. The spirit is willing, but the flesh is weak." (Matt 26:36–41)

We might say that Jesus prayed alone in this passage. But his disciples are there with him. He has gone out a little bit from them, but they are close enough that he asks them why they couldn't keep watch for a mere hour. They were praying separately, but they were also together in the garden. The disciples were supposed to be with Jesus praying and watching.

When we think of sanctification as primarily an individual event, we can marginalize God's family and end up with a perverted view of Christianity. Someone can memorize the Bible but not know how to live out what the Bible teaches. We can understand all of the doctrines of the church, but not love our brother or sister. When we do things with the church as the church, we learn not only the content of our Christian faith, but also the praxis of our faith. As James writes, "Show me your faith without deeds, and I will show you my faith by my deeds" (Jas 2:18).

We learn things we cannot grasp alone by experience in the church. I can learn that I should forgive my brother or sister when they wrong me by reading what Jesus taught. I can also learn that I should forgive them again if they wrong me again by studying the Bible. While I might be able to learn these things in private prayer time, I cannot learn to forgive my brother or sister until I experience the slight or insult. In other words, I can learn about forgiveness alone, but I can only learn to forgive with others. Similarly, I can learn about loving my church family in private devotional time. I will only actually love my family if I spend time with them and get to know them.

Too often we confuse the idea of learning about sanctification with the actual process of sanctification. We can learn all about the things we need to do to become more like Jesus, but we don't experience sanctification until we actually do those things. Until we have relationships where we have to live Jesus' teachings, we won't make any progress. The church aids us in the sanctification process because it is the place where we get to practice what we learn. We can practice much of the Christian life outside the church as well, but the church is the place God designed for Christians to become sanctified together.

Providence: Directing the Family

God is working to provide and direct his family so that it will accomplish his purposes and become the community he has intended. Providence describes the way that God interacts with his creation. Different views of providence lead to different views of human freedom. Regardless of which view of providence one takes, we should all agree that God directs his family through complex human interactions and situations.

God directs his family by bringing us into relationships with others who will shape us and provide experiences needed to form our character. If I am too trusting, God may bring me into contact with someone who is not very trustworthy. Experiencing someone who cannot be trusted may help me become more discerning in future relationships. God may also have brought the person who was not trustworthy into contact with me to shape them and make them more sensitive to those who are somewhat naive. God might do this so that they may be more open and honest in future encounters.

We know very little about the complex interrelations between human actions and God's plan. But we know that God is working to bring about his will in the world. We also know that he uses the church. With this in mind, we know that God uses the situations we experience to shape us into the people he desires us to be. Although we may question any particular situation we find ourselves in, we trust that God is able to use the totality of our experiences so that his will is accomplished. Christians are confident in God's providential directing, even if we don't understand how God is accomplishing his will, and even if we cannot see how his will is being accomplished.

Prayer: Communicating as a Family

Praying with others is a powerful experience. When God's family prays together, we benefit not only from our own prayers, but also from the prayers of our brothers and sisters. Prayers at churches are often a single person praying on behalf of the group or congregation. This is not a bad thing, but this is not the kind of prayer I am referring to as a powerful experience.

When the church family comes together and prays for one another and with one another we have the ability to experience God's love and direction in ways not available when praying alone. A common way to pray in relatively small groupings is to share with one another our concerns and praises, and then to have a time for each person to voice a prayer for the group. This kind of self-revealing builds trust between the members of the group. When others voice prayers for our concerns and when we do likewise we have the opportunity to hear our own concerns voiced to God by another. God can use the act of having another person pray for us to provide insight and answers to our own prayers.

It is not unusual for people who are sharing needs within a church to find that God has provided the means of meeting the particular need by someone who is in the very group that is preparing to pray. We should not be surprised that God would have a need met by someone who is hearing the request being voiced. God is proactive in answering our prayers, and he knows our needs before we know them.

In addition to meeting needs in prayer, God can speak to us and through us when we pray as a family. If I am in turmoil, the act of me hearing another Christian pray for my peace may be the very thing God uses to grant me that peace. When I pray for someone to have courage, God may use the way I voice that prayer to provide the courage they need. As Christians, we understand that God is in our midst when we gather. In addition, the Holy Spirit indwells believers and prays for us with groaning we cannot understand. When we pray together, not only are we praying, but the Holy Spirit is also praying with each of us. It should be no surprise that we often experience a powerful manifestation of God when we pray as a group of Christians. If God is praying with each of us as we are praying, that is a lot of power.

Although we can pray alone, and there may be many times when we have to pray alone, we should seek to maximize the amount of time we have to pray as the family of God. Dedicated time to pray together has the opportunity to be a powerful force in the life of the church and in our individual lives. Corporate prayers, in large groups and small groups, are tremendous benefits of being a part of God's family, the church.

Service: Working Together as a Family

Working together with other believers in the service of God is fulfilling and part of our purpose. Human relationships grow stronger when we share common tasks. Those who work alongside one another for long periods of time develop close relationships. When people collaborate to complete tasks, they learn about one another. When working together, you can find out how dedicated your partners are to the job. Workers also discuss issues they are dealing with in their own lives while working or during breaks. Trust also develops between people who work together, particularly in jobs that have an element of danger.

In addition to the connections and sharing that come from common labor, people also share a sense of pride and accomplishment in completing tasks. When constructing a building, the group can come together and admire that which they built. Each person knows that they contributed to the construction, and that the task would not be complete if they had not participated.

Connections through shared goals and labor build strong bonds between people. Service in the family of God is the same. Serving God by serving the church allows people the same kinds of opportunities to bond with one another. Working with a fellow believer to take care of an older member of the congregation allows those serving to help the older member work together and build the bonds that form from shared labor. In addition, the member who is being served is able to bond with those who are serving (at least, in some cases).

Working together in the service of the church allows us to see tangible results of our service to God. As the congregation has needs that are being met by the other members of the congregation, we are able to have a sense that we are caring for one another. As church ministries are carried out by members, we can join in the sense of accomplishment that we are doing the things God has called us to do. When we reflect on the various accomplishments of the church, we can see that we had a part in the church attaining its goal.

The bonds that draw us together in shared labor and purpose allow us to experience God laboring beside us as we labor beside fellow believers. Since Christians are indwelt by the Holy Spirit, we are, in a real sense, working along with God when we work together. Not only is God working in us, but in the other believers we are working with. God is working in us and around us when we labor together with other believers in God's service.

THE CHURCH AS GOD'S FAMILY

God has been interested in humans since he created them. Throughout the Bible, we find that God has had special relationships with certain people. One of the major components of the Old Testament is that God has a special people who are in a covenant relationship with him. The Hebrew people, Israel, are God's own special people. God has special plans for Israel and brings them into a special land of his own choosing.

Over time, his people have periods of drawing close to God and honoring their covenant, as well as periods of falling away from God and abandoning the covenant. God brings judgment on his people so that they will return to him when they go astray. Out from God's covenant community a messiah is promised. This messiah will bring God's people into a better and more stable relationship with him. The messiah will rule like David and restore the glory to God's people.

God Founded the church

It is within the grand view of Jewish history that a poor Jewish couple has a child. The child was not unexpected—he had been announced by an angel from God—but his nature was a surprise. Out of the blue, young Mary is told that she will give birth to the Messiah. God had been silent for four hundred years; but now, God has announced the arrival of the Messiah. Joseph, a young laborer who probably worked with stone, will raise the messiah as his own son, though he will not be his father. Mary will conceive and give birth to the Messiah, though she is a virgin and will remain a virgin until Jesus is born.

At long last, Jesus is born, and the heavens themselves announce his coming. Men from far off read the signs in the stars and recognized that a unique event is taking place. A king of kings is coming into the world, and so they followed the signs to the land occupied by God's people, Israel. Unusual circumstances surrounded the announcement that Jesus would be born, and they continue as precious gifts are given by powerful people to the poor young family. Joseph is warned in a dream to flee to Egypt for the safety of his family, and he does. Eventually Jesus' family is able to return home and they live a life that is probably fairly normal. One exception is found when the family loses Jesus in Jerusalem for a few days when he was twelve.

Jesus eventually comes on the scene as an adult and is baptized by his cousin. He gathers disciples and begins to teach them about God and perform signs and wonders that demonstrate that he is the Messiah. The religious leadership of Israel is threatened by Jesus. His teaching rings true, but is different than what they have been taught. The people are attracted to him, and he draws crowds. Jesus begins to claim that he has a special relationship with God, and people wonder if he could be the long-awaited Messiah. The religious leadership fears an uprising of the people against Rome. They know a revolution would be disastrous for Israel.

The Jewish religious leadership plots to have the agitator killed and they succeed. Jesus is crucified outside of Jerusalem and dies. His body is removed from the cross and placed in a tomb. On the third day, some of his followers find his tomb empty, and eventually see him, alive again, having been resurrected. Jesus' followers go from despair and mourning to joy. Shortly after the resurrection, the church is born.

Out of God's people, the nation of Israel, comes Jesus the Messiah. Jesus teaches the Israelites that the genuine way to be part of God's family is to accept him as being from God and join his new community. The Messiah births the church from his followers. The church grows from a small band of Jews to an international movement of Jesus' followers that spans the globe.

The church is founded by Jesus, who is himself divine. The church is rooted in the nation of Israel, whom God had selected as his own people. God is responsible for the establishment of the church. God started the church with Jesus' followers and allowed it to grow and prosper throughout the years.

Each person who becomes a Christian joins this band of Jesus followers. Although the church has looked different over the years, it has remained the same. At the head of the church is Jesus, who directs his people through the Holy Spirit. All of the church's members have been adopted into God's family and are indwelt by the Spirit. God leads them to fulfill his plan in their lives and in the life of the church. The church is filled with God's children, and is God's plan for revealing himself to the creation and for accomplishing his work on earth.

God Empowered and Organized the Church

God started the church and he empowered it. He guides his people through the structures of the church. The Bible contains revelation of God that he has intended the church to use throughout the centuries. Christians have utilized Scripture since the beginning of the church to help them understand how they are to live and function as God's people.

The Bible contains much information about how Christians should order their lives, as well as the way early Christians lived and encountered the world that was often hostile to their message. Some of the information about the things the early church did are descriptive. That is to say, the Bible records how they interacted with the world, but is not instructing other Christians that they should do the same things.

As an example, consider when Peter is told to go to Cornelius. The book of Acts records that Peter receives a vision from God and then goes to meet a Roman soldier. While he is with Cornelius, Peter comes to understand that gentiles are also accepted by God and can become Christians. This account of Peter's ministry is obviously descriptive. Christians never expected to receive visions and go meet with Roman soldiers. This passage does not teach us that we should all have a vision from God and then go meet with our "Cornelius." This passage simply describes something that happened.

Although this passage is descriptive, we can learn from it. The minimum we should learn is what Peter learns about God accepting gentiles. Beyond that, we can also learn some other things. Prior to this event, Peter did not believe that the gospel was available to the gentiles. He formed his opinion because of his religious upbringing. However, God intervened to change Peter's perspective on gentiles because, contrary to what Peter had been taught, God accepted them. Beyond the specific teaching about gentiles, we can also learn that God will sometimes change our views when they are wrong. We may form opinions about religious matters that are contrary to God's plan. God may very well intervene in our lives to correct us when we are wrong.

While descriptive passages tell us what happened without expecting us to try to recreate the situations or pattern our behavior after what we read, the Bible also contains prescriptive passages. Prescriptive teachings were written as a guide for our behavior. When Jesus commands his church to go and make disciples, he expects us to obey. Prescriptive teachings have an expectation that we will do what the author is telling us to do.

The Bible is a wealth of information for Christians and for the church. It contains descriptions of certain events in the history of God's people. We can learn from these stories. The Bible also contains teachings that we are expected to follow. Both types of passages inform, educate, and guide the church. The Scriptures have been a source of inspiration and empowerment for the church from the earliest times. God has used his word to organize and empower his church.

The church is an organization of humans in service to God, and Jesus himself is the head of the church. Although we currently do not encounter Jesus in the same way that his disciples did when he led them on the Earth, we do still encounter him. He is the ultimate leader of the church. As the leader of the church, we are to seek his will and direction. Jesus leads his church through his people. He uses his followers to lead his church. God may lead someone by shaping their life circumstances or by drawing them in a particular direction. He uses the Scriptures and the prayers of his people to give light to the path the church should take.

The church is led by Jesus, but unfortunately she does not always follow very well. Just like the Israelites had a problem remaining focused on and faithful to God, the church also struggles to follow Jesus' lead. Sometimes

God's People

congregations have lost their way and have ceased to function as a church. Other times congregations have served their purpose and died. Jesus is always leading his church; sometimes the congregations simply do not follow. However, when Jesus is followed faithfully, the church is functioning as it should, and Christians begin to experience sanctification and look more like Jesus. The church becomes closer to God because, as a whole, the people are moving closer to God as individuals.

Although Jesus is the ultimate head of the church, it does have human leaders. God selected the leaders of the church in the past and continues to select leaders today. The first disciples were called by Jesus himself; they became the first leaders in the church. Since Jesus is divine, we can see clearly how God chose the first generation of leadership. We have their stories of how they we called to service in the Bible itself. Subsequent generations of leadership have followed, and we do not have their calling into ministry recorded in the Bible.

God continues to call people to serve him. God raises people of every generation to serve his church, and he will continue to do so. The call to serve in ministry is a personal call. There are no telegrams from heaven that announce who God has selected to serve him. God calls individuals through their own life experience and the situations he takes them through. Sometimes a person's call to serve is clear and immediate. Other times, the road is longer and has many subtle signposts that eventually make the destination of a life in God's service clear. Regardless of how God calls someone into his service, God does do so.

People hear God's call in its varied forms and respond in different ways. The best way is to submit to God's will and follow. Some refuse and miss out on blessings. Christians ought to be careful to listen for God when he is leading us so that we can serve him in whatever capacity he desires. Whether we serve God in a vocational church position or as a member of the laity, we should seek to be where God wants us to be.

Sometimes people may seek to serve God in a place that he has not called them. Churches may affirm a call that is not present in an individual and give them positions within the church that they should not have. Some people who are in leadership positions within God's church not have been called by God to serve in those positions. Sometimes they may not be believers. When nonbelievers are in positions of leadership, bad things can happen. Bad things can also happen when believers serve in a position where God has not called them. Churches and individuals must be careful to ensure that people are actually following God's call and that people are serving in the places that God has actually called them. When the church has in place the leaders God has intended, it will function more like God intends for it to function. As I have written before, when the church is functioning more like it should, the people will experience sanctification and the entire church will become closer to God.

Finally, the church has the Holy Spirit all throughout the congregation. As the Holy Spirit indwells each believer, he guides all of the members of the church to accomplish their tasks. When the church relies on the supernatural guidance of the Spirit, the people will accomplish what God has intended.

The church has Jesus at the head, the Scriptures as a steady guide and reference, divinely chosen leadership on the front lines, and the indwelling of the Holy Spirit to empower it. God is all over his church. God empowers and leads his church in every way the church can be led. If God is all over the church, then it makes sense that the best way to be close to God is to be in and close to his church.

THE CHURCH IS GOD'S VISIBLE FAMILY ON EARTH

The church is precious to God. The Father ordained the church, the Son died for the church, and the Holy Spirit indwells the church. We know of no other grouping of people or organization that God uses in the way he uses the church. The church is the main way that God brings about his will on Earth. Through the ministries and individuals of the church, God accomplishes his will in the world. Jesus took on flesh when he was born in Jerusalem, and he reigns as the Incarnate Son. We might also think of the church as God taking on humanity again, though in a different way.

Because believers are indwelt by the Holy Spirit, in some sense we might think of the Holy Spirit as being incarnate within the people of the church. We should not confuse the presence of the Holy Spirit in the church with the incarnation of Jesus, since the incarnation of Jesus was very different. When Jesus took on humanity, he became something he was not (human) while remaining divine. When we think of the Holy Spirit as being incarnate through the church, I am noting that the work of the Holy Spirit is primarily performed in the human members of the church. As the Holy Spirit indwells individuals and leads them to perform his will, the Spirit can be seen as acting through the actions of humans.

When God's family is in submission to God's will and working according to his plan, its accomplishments can be seen as the Holy Spirit's accomplishments. This is not to minimize the role of humans in the work of the church, but to realize that God is also at work in the church. God uses his family as both agents and instruments to accomplish his will. While humans are the ones performing the tasks of ministry within the church, God is also working in and with humans to accomplish those tasks. We might then view the actions of the church, when it is in submission to God's will, as God's actions through his family.

If it is true that we should view the actions of the church as God's actions through the church, then answering the question "what has God done lately?" is very easy. If you want to see what God has done, look at what his family has done. The church is serving God and accomplishing his will on Earth. To the degree that the church is faithfully executing God's will, we can say that God is working in the world.

For the critic who claims the Bible has records of God acting in the ancient world but we do not see God doing anything today, we can claim the contrary. In fact, given the numerical and geographical expansion of Christianity throughout the globe, we can say with confidence that God is acting visibly in the world more now than at any time in the past. The advancing of the church is the advancing of God working throughout the world. Dominion of creation is taking place by humans (as God intended with Adam), but also by God himself indwelling his church.

The idea that God's actions should be seen only as supernatural phenomena that defies explanation is absurd. Many of God's actions as recorded in the Bible were through the actions of his people. Occasionally, we have recorded a spectacular supernatural event, and we are drawn to them. The parting of seas and rivers, walking on water, and bushes that burn and are not consumed are amazing, and we may long to behold such events. It is foolish, however, to think that God's action is restricted to such amazing instances. God can work in the little things just as he can work in the big things. It is no less God's action when he leads his people through small and ordinary occurrences than it would be for him to have a supernatural banner in the sky with bulleted instructions. We may like the idea of supernatural signposts, because we long to have exciting encounters of the supernatural, but it is unfair to say that God is not leading his people unless he is leading them in a way that we like or prefer.

God, the first person of the Trinity, is referred to as Father, and Jesus, the second person of the Trinity, as the Son. Christians become adopted siblings of Jesus and one another. Christians make up the church. The church is the primary way that God interacts with the world. While God is free to perform supernatural acts outside of his family, those type of actions do not appear to be common. The typical way that God accomplishes his will on Earth is through his visible family, the church.

Chapter Six

Encountering God through the Church

THE CHURCH HAS CERTAIN functions to perform. Wayne Grudem, in his Systematic Theology, claims that the church has a threefold purpose, which he describes as ministry to God, believers, and the world. I like his categories, and I have used them for some time in discussions of the things the church should be about. In this section, I use his basic template, but I have expanded and refined the contents of his categories.

ADORATION: MINISTRY TO GOD

Ministry to God is the first purpose of the church. The church is to adore God. As a church, we adore God in different ways. Personal prayer and worship is one such way. We are instructed to worship God as a corporate body, however, and we should not reduce our adoration of God to a primarily personal event.

God is due all glory, honor, praise, and worship. The church should gather on a regular basis to perform acts of adoration as a family. Churches do gather on a regular basis to perform these activities, usually on Sundays. Adoration of God includes worship, giving, and observance of the ordinances of the church (baptism and communion). Believers encounter God when they adore him.

Worship

> Let the message of Christ dwell among you richly as you teach and admonish one another with all wisdom through psalms, hymns, and songs from the Spirit, singing to God with gratitude in your hearts. (Col 3:16)

Singing Together

Current discussion of worship tends to refer to music almost exclusively. Music, in particular God's people singing, can be part of worship, but we should not think that worship is reduced to singing or music. Worship is the act of attributing worth to God. This can be accomplished in any number of ways. Singing is a common and enjoyable way to worship. Songs that glorify God have ever been upon the lips of his people. Many people feel closer to God when they are praising him through song. We often encounter God when we sing together as his people.

Praying Together

Worship also includes praying. God's people should pray together. Prayers should not only be petitions (when we ask God to give us things), but they should also be praise and exaltation. Praying to God is an act of worship (since we acknowledge his greatness and our dependence upon him). Asking God to grant you something you cannot do for yourself is humbling yourself before him. Telling God of his greatness in prayer is directly attributing worth to God. Knowing that the Holy Spirit prays with us when we pray and knowing that praying as group of Christians means that the Holy Spirit is also praying with all of the believers involved should remind us that we are encountering God in a powerful way.

Reading Scripture Together

Reading Scripture together is another way to worship God. God's word is powerful and accomplishes what he intends for it to accomplish (Isa 55:11). One of the defining characteristics of early Christian worship was the reading of God's word. Prior to the advent of the printing press, copies of Scriptures were expensive and not readily available to Christians. Since

Gutenberg invented his printing press, copies of the Bible have become more available to God's people. In addition, the literacy rate has also increased. In the past, relatively few people could read, but literacy is now common in many places.

Combine an increase in the literacy rate with readily available copies of the Bible and we have access to God's word in ways that would be unbelievable just a few centuries ago. However, since reading the Bible in public was seen as a necessity in the past because people could not read it on their own, Scripture reading in worship services is less common today than in most of our Christian history. The church is not better off by jettisoning public Scripture reading and simply encouraging private Scripture reading.

When we read God's word as a church family, we all encounter it together. Certain passages, particularly those that tell us we should be doing something together, are powerful when read in a corporate setting. The words of Jesus in John 13 are an example of this: "A new command I give you: Love one another. As I have loved you, so you must love one another. By this everyone will know that you are my disciples, if you love one another" (John 13:34–35). While we may be able to understand the content of this verse while we read it alone with a cup of coffee, the experience of reading this verse with the very people we are supposed to love can elicit a much more profound response, especially when we may be sitting next to someone that we may not like. God's word can confront us in corporate settings differently that it might when we are sitting alone in quiet contemplation. The world we live in is messy. People around us sometimes knock us off balance, physically and emotionally. God's word is just as powerful, if not more powerful, when we are among those we are supposed to be loving and when we may not feel much like loving them.

Passages that tell us we (as a group) are something in Christ are also profoundly powerful in group settings. For example, "But you are a chosen people, a royal priesthood, a holy nation, God's special possession, that you may declare the praises of him who called you out of darkness into his wonderful light. Once you were not a people, but now you are the people of God; once you had not received mercy, but now you have received mercy" (1 Pet 2:9–10). A public reading of this passage can have a profound effect on how we view ourselves, not just as individuals, but as the church family. When this passage is being read and contemplated in the company of other believers, we may view our church family a bit differently. I may come to realize that not only have I been chosen as part of a royal priesthood, but so has the rest of our church family. A greater sense of reverence and love for our brothers and sisters may come about because of a public reading of this passage. Similar responses may not happen if we read Scripture in isolation. In fact, we may internalize this passage with only ourselves in view and develop a perverted sense of pride by failing to see the application to the larger church.

God's people are drawn closer to him and closer to one another through the public reading of Scripture. Scripture can be read in unison, with everyone reading the same passage together aloud. It can also be read by a single person while the rest of the congregation listens and reflects on it. Finally, Scripture can be read responsively. In a responsive reading, a leader reads a portion of the text, and the congregation reads another portion in response. All of these ways to read Scripture together are beneficial for the church and allow people to encounter God through his word and through his people.

Proclaiming God's Word Together

Another way we worship together is by proclaiming God's word together. This includes hearing God's word proclaimed, what we commonly call a sermon. Following in the footsteps of the prophets, the apostles, and Jesus himself, we proclaim God's word publicly as part of our worship. In the proclamation of God's word, we announce what God has declared and expound upon its meaning and application for the church.

Scripture belongs to the church (corporately) and is a foundation of our identity. Preaching should have its focus on the corporate body that is the church, and should not be thought of as self-improvement. While becoming more sanctified as individuals is a natural consequence of living as the church, the proclamation of God's word should be primarily an act of worship and only secondarily a teaching time. Teaching that happens in the course of a sermon should be incidental to the call of the church to exalt God and humble themselves before him. The teaching of God's word should take place outside of worship.

Proclamation of God's word should serve as a conduit to connect the congregation with the heart of God. Similarly to the way Christians can encounter God by reading his word together, hearing God's word proclaimed and expounded together should draw believers closer to God. God's word not only read, but explained and applied, should spur Christians to live more along the lines that God has set before us.

Encounters of God through Worship

Worship is a dynamic experience. Christians have the privilege of participating in corporate worship of God. When we worship God properly using the elements described above, our lives should be changed and we should become more sanctified. Three things happen to believers when we worship God as we should. First, we find joy in God. Humans are creatures built to worship God and find delight in him. When we worship God properly, we find that what David wrote was true: "You will fill me with joy in your presence" (Ps 16:11). Coming into God's presence as a group of believers gives us a glimpse of our ultimate goal, living in God's presence. We have the opportunity to experience a part of that glorious future in the present. Joy should be a natural byproduct of encountering God in worship.

Second, we draw near to God and God draws near to us. James writes, "Come near to God and he will come near to you" (Jas 4:8). The gathering of a group of Christians in unity to worship God together can be viewed as a concentration of God's presence. While God is present everywhere at all times (omnipresence), there is something unique about Christians gathering together, since all believers are indwelt by the Holy Spirit. A corporate worship gathering can be thought of as coming close to God in the senses that worshipers are orienting themselves toward God and doing what we were created to do, and that when indwelt believers gather together in one place, the spirit of God is present in each believer in a special way. All of the synergistic aspects of Christians functioning together in unison and according to God's will are expressed in corporate worship. Corporate worship draws Christians closer to God and one another in dramatically powerful ways.

Third, God ministers to us in worship. Although worship is for God, we are changed as we encounter God in worship. "Let us approach the throne of grace with confidence, so that we may receive mercy and find grace to help us in our time of need" (Heb 4:16). God desires and deserves our worship, but he does not need it. Worship is a chance for us to experience his love for us and for us to experience how we should function as creatures and as children. God accepts worship from us, though it is imperfect. More than just accepting our worship, God actually gives us mercy and grace in our worship. Some of that mercy and grace, no doubt, is in his acceptance of imperfect and impure worship, but it also extends to our other needs as well. Humans are needy creatures and God meets those needs in many ways. One way is in our worship of him.

Worshiping God as a corporate body is a great privilege for the church. We should seek to make sure our worship is appropriate, which is a subject for another time. We should enjoy our worship of God and come away from it having encountered God in the praises of his people. If we are not encountering God in this way, we should evaluate what we are doing and make whatever changes are needed to ensure that God's people encounter God in worship.

Giving

> But who am I, and who are my people, that we should be able to give as generously as this? Everything comes from you, and we have given you only what comes from your hand. (1 Chr 29:14)

Giving from what God has given to us is an act of worship. We may not get excited when the topic of giving comes up, but we should remember that God is glorified and worshiped in our tithes and offerings. In the Old Testament, we find that God commanded a tithe from his people. The tithe did not even belong to the people, it belonged to God (Lev 27:30). When the people brought in this tithe, they were simply returning to God something that they did not have any claim on in the first place.

When we hold loosely to our material possessions and realize that what we give to God is returning a portion of what he gave to us in the first place, it is easier to give. When we see our giving, our presentation of the firstfruits (the best of what we have) as part of our worship, we can view giving as a privilege, not an obligation. Being cheerful in our giving (2 Cor 9:7) indicates that we see our giving as worship that will be accepted by God.

While we sometimes talk about giving as an opportunity to participate in keeping the ministries funded and keeping the lights on at the church, we should not primarily see giving through the lens of what it accomplishes. When we view giving in pragmatic ways, we tend to see the gift as a tool. If our gifts are tools, then we may want to have more control over the way those tools are used. Sometimes people give gifts to the church with strings attached. Giving with strings is not a good way to give. The thing about giving a tithe or offering is that, particularly in the Old Testament, they were consumed by the priests. When you brought a lamb to be sacrificed, it would be slaughtered and eaten. Giving with strings attached is not a good model because we attempt to manipulate the use of gifts, which is asserting the right to control them after they are given. As we have discussed previously, we should not take that which belongs to God. In the case of giving, strings attached to our gifts can serve as taking prerogative that belongs to God, with respect to the use of gifts, for ourselves.

Proper giving to God is an act of worship that allows us to encounter God. As we give, we show gratitude to God for the blessings he has entrusted to us. Showing gratitude to God for our blessings indicates a realization that we are dependent on God and submissive to his will. Submitting to God's will and obediently acting in accordance with his will is progress toward sanctification. As we become more sanctified, we have a closer relationship with God, and therefore encounter God better.

Baptism and Communion

Throughout the history of the church, Christians have observed rites that identified them with the church and signified aspects of the common faith. Two of these rites, baptism and communion (also known as the Lords' Supper or the Eucharist), are shared, to one degree or another, by all who share the common Christian faith. Although different Christian traditions view these two rites with differing degrees of meaning and emphasis, all see them as Christian rituals of significance.

Baptism and communion are given by Jesus to his church. Christians are expected to participate in them, and they should be viewed as elements of worship. I do not mean that baptism and communion should only be observed in or as part of a designated time of worship. I mean that the act of baptism and the act of communion are themselves worship of God. The ordinances of the church are just as much worship as are singing, praying, reading Scripture, proclaiming God's word, and giving.

God is worshiped in baptism because we are signifying in a very public way our submission to God and trust in him. We may sing of our submission to God and our trust in him. We may pray for and confess those things in prayer. We may read them from the Bible and hear them preached in worship. The act of baptism is a visible and physical demonstration of our identification with Jesus and his church. We worship God in the act of baptism. Baptism, however, is a one-time act of worship. Unlike the other elements mentioned, we do not repeat baptism on a regular basis. The fact that it is a singly observed ordinance does not make it any less worship.

Communion is similar to baptism in that it is a visible and physical act of worship that shows submission to Christ and identification with his church. The act of partaking of the elements of communion speaks of our remembrance of Jesus' sacrifice for us, our current fellowship with him and his church, and the anticipatory aspect of a future celebration with Jesus in his kingdom. Unlike baptism, communion is repeated on a regular basis.

While most acts of worship are primarily verbal, baptism and communion are nonverbal acts of worship. Giving is also not a verbal action, but involves parting with physical blessings. These aspects of worship help to connect the entire human person to God in worship. If not for physical aspects of worship, we might see worship as primarily a mental action. We should not. We are not merely mental beings. We are able to worship God with all that we are. As humans, we have aspects of our existence that are mental and physical. We also have an aspect of our existence in which we exercise dominion over a part of the physical world. God has provided ways for us to worship him in all three realms of our being. When we worship God holistically (mentally, physically, and through our dominion) we are sanctified and encounter God more fully.

NURTURING: MINISTRY TO THE CHURCH

Ministry to God's family is the next purpose of the church. The church ministers to itself through fellowship and teaching. By its very nature, fellowship is a social activity and makes the church healthier. Genuine fellowship should go beyond weekly meetings and planned events at the church campus. Believers who invest in the lives of others over extended periods of time display the type of relationships the church should foster. These relationships will seek to meet needs and provide correction when a member strays from the family. Teaching within the church also serves to make the church healthier. As a church becomes healthier and provides a nurturing environment for believers, people are able to encounter God better.

Teaching

Within the family of God, there is much to learn. From the content and application of Scripture to church history, apologetics, evangelism, missions, and other topics, learning and experiences must be communicated from mature members to the younger ones. The church needs to mature its members and build up the body of Christ. In Colossians, Paul writes, "He is the one we proclaim, admonishing and teaching everyone with all wisdom, so that we may present everyone fully mature in Christ" (Col 1:28). Paul values teaching so that the church will become mature. New members come into the family with a lack of knowledge and a level of immaturity. While people are not expected to come to Christ fully mature, they are expected to grow in maturity. One of the jobs of the church is to provide the teaching needed so that they can grow and become fully mature in Christ.

Teaching should also prepare people to serve. Paul also writes about the need to edify the church, "to equip his people for works of service, so that the body of Christ may be built up until we all reach unity in the faith and in the knowledge of the Son of God and become mature, attaining to the whole measure of the fullness of Christ" (Eph 4:12–13). In this passage, building up the church has the goal of unity, maturity, and the fullness of Christ. Paul is an advocate of teaching within the church.

A major goal of teaching is maturity of the believers. We have already discussed this concept as sanctification. All teaching should have the goal of leading believers to become more like Christ. Much of the teaching content provided by the church is information and has to be internalized and acted upon before it provides the desired sanctification. Within the church setting, there must be an eye toward how the things learned are applied and lived out. Some topics are more difficult than others, but what we believe influences the choices we make, so we should make connections between abstract concepts and how they affect behavior whenever possible.

Teaching Scriptures Together

The church must teach the Scriptures. The Bible contains the revelation of God to his people. Reading Scripture together is important in worship, and teaching the Scriptures together is important for maturing the church.

Bible study can be done alone, and many people take personal time to study. The church should also provide opportunities to teach the Bible to its members so that there is a measure of oversight for proper teaching. From small-group Bible studies to mentoring programs and from technology-enhanced delivery systems to lecture-hall-style classes, the church has options in the way it delivers the needed study of the Scriptures.

Learning the Bible as a group allows for questions and insight from the students. Teachers, even experienced ones, need feedback from their students to assess how well the material being studied is understood. Studying alone can provide vast quantities of information, but does not provide opportunities for correction if something is misunderstood. Group learning also allows for screening of the material being used. Many resources available are of poor quality, or have gross misinterpretations or even heresy.

Bible studies, when properly led and supervised, provide a safe place to examine the Scriptures, even the difficult passages. They can also provide proper hermeneutical guidelines for examining the ancient biblical texts. Hermeneutics, the discipline of interpretation, is vital for properly understanding what God has preserved in his word. The church should assist believers in developing good approaches to the text and good habits for study.

Teaching Doctrines Together

The Scriptures are vital because they are God's revelation, and because they systematize and explain the teachings of the Bible and how they relate to the world. In a sense, doctrines summarize and expand on what the Bible teaches.

The Bible teaches that God is powerful. Christian doctrine describes God's power as omnipotence, and theologians explore and define its limits. The Bible teaches that God possesses knowledge. Christian doctrine describes God's knowledge as omniscience, and theologians explore and define its limits. The Bible teaches that there is a single God, and that the Father, Son, and Holy Spirit are unique persons who are each divine. Christian doctrine describes God as Trinity, and theologians explore and define God's unity, the personhood of each member of the Trinity, and function of each member within creation.

Some of the doctrines of the church are loaded with philosophical content, and others are not. Learning theology alone is possible, but it is a task done best with an experienced guide. The well-worn trails of Christian doctrine pass near deep chasms in which people can get lost and hurt. Unfortunately, some people simply put up warning signs and tell people to stay away. While that may help some avoid the potential danger, it is not a good practice. Some of the chasms have grand views, and explorers need to get close to the edge and take in the scenery, as it helps us to understand the world around us. Rather than simply telling people to avoid difficult issues, the church should provide experienced guides to walk people through the precarious places. A faith that can't stand up to tough questions is itself a questionable faith. Christianity can withstand inquiry, and the church should be as prepared as it can be when confronted by skeptics.

Just as Bible studies should have proper supervision from church leadership, doctrinal studies should also have proper oversight. There is a lot of bad theology out there. In addition, different church traditions have different confessional documents, and consequently different doctrinal positions. The church should take seriously the need to provide doctrinal teaching for its members.

Teaching History Together

Teaching history together is also important. While the potential pitfalls of individual Bible study and doctrinal study are not as severe, church history does have its own unique set of challenges for a novice student. In one sense, the history of the church begins with the book of Acts in the Bible. Early personalities and events are chronicled in Acts, but it is also Scripture. Other New Testament writings contain some historical details, but again, they are themselves Scripture. For this reason, another way to look at the beginning of the history of the church is to focus on the non-Scriptural resources and focus on the time after the writing of the New Testament documents.

The church has an interesting history and has events and decisions that may cause unease for a believer. Just as the Gospels show us that Jesus' disciples were men who made mistakes, church history shows us that those leading the church have also been men who have made mistakes. Sometimes the mistakes were minor, and other times they were major and egregious. Sometimes the church seems to be motivated for reasons that are not particularly spiritual, and perhaps downright earthly.

The church has persisted, and her history is our own. We cannot stick our heads in the sand, nor can we gloss over the checkered history of God's family. We should not try to avoid our history. We have no reason to avoid our history. As believers, we owe a debt of gratitude for our faith to those who have come before. Whether they lived two thousand years ago or two years ago, they came before us and brought the church to the place it is today. We need to learn from our history so that we can appreciate our heritage and those who came before. We also need to learn our history so that we can better lead the church in our time. Understanding how the church navigated the difficulties of the past may help us avoid the potholes of our present and future.

As with Bible studies and doctrinal studies, studying church history is best done with a guide. The guide should be able to point out the shameful decisions and events made in our past, as well as the laudatory decisions and events. Showing the shared heritage and shared challenges experienced by those who came before can help us have confidence in God. Jesus is still at the head of the church—he always has been and always will. Understanding our history may help us cling more closely to him as we follow into the future.

Teaching How to Live as Christians Together

The church is a social institution and a living organism. Difficulty and blessings arise from the persons within the local body of Christ. Knowing how I should treat others is very different from treating someone the way I should. The knowledge acquired through Bible studies, doctrinal studies, and church history benefit the church and the individual when applied to interpersonal relationships within the church. The church must teach its members how to live the Christian life together.

The world is a complicated place, and it shows no signs of simplifying anytime soon. The church is filled with people who have difficulty integrating what we teach into their lives. It is very frustrating to know that I should model Jesus' love at home, but not know how to do it. Parents can become overwhelmed knowing that they should help their child learn to forgive when they themselves struggle to forgive. Aside from uniquely Christian teachings, some people need to learn basic life skills, because for whatever reason they are unable to do certain things like balance a checkbook, make a budget, cook a healthy meal, or change the oil in their car.

The church should identify the issues the particular congregation faces and develop ways to help their members learn what they need so they can function well within the church. Issues are as varied as the people in our churches. One church may need classes on raising children, while another church needs to teach its members how to raise food. One church may need to teach newlyweds how to love and support each other, while another may need to teach seniors how to cope with dementia or loss of function. One church may need to teach their members how to be good friends, and another may need to teach basic home repair. Each church family is different and will have different needs and different resources available. Churches should use what they have to meet the needs they have as effectively as they can.

Teaching Methodologies

Teaching can take place in many different forms. Technology has expanded and will continue to expand the avenues available to get information to people. Churches should use technology, but we should remember that there is an aspect of learning that needs interaction. The goal of learning in the church is not the same as learning in a college or graduate school. In the church, application of what we learn should happen now, not at some point in the future. Assessment of the learning is not gauged in tests or papers, but in living out the teachings. Sanctification is the ultimate goal.

With sanctification in mind, teaching within the church should move people toward action more than reflection. Reflection is good, but action is better. When we teach about forgiveness, we should include, as much as we can, the practice of forgiving. When we teach that love covers a multitude of sin, we should help them to begin to love those in the church who have wronged them. The church is not the academy where we ponder the implications of our faith, but rather the proving grounds where we put our faith into practice.

Fellowship

Mature believers have good relationships with others. They have learned how to think of others first and put themselves last. The way that we develop that kind of care and love for one another is to spend time together. We should spend time together at organized church functions, and we should spend even more time outside of them.

Friendships require effort. Acquaintances can develop at church activities. Developing friendships takes more than just coming to church together. Our church should value friendship and provide times for members to become friends through social activities at our facilities and elsewhere.

Close friendships persist even through difficult times. When we genuinely care about someone, we provide correction when they are doing something wrong or destructive. Love can sometimes be tough, in that it wants what is best for the other person, not just what may be the easiest or most pleasurable. When the church has healthy fellowship and the people genuinely love one another, people can encounter God's love through the love of the congregation.

Sharing Life Together

Jesus called disciples to follow him, and they spent a lot of time together. Over the short period of time Jesus had a public ministry, he likely was with his disciples for more hours than two people who attend the same church may spend together over twenty years. If Jesus had called his disciples to follow him, like many of our churches call people to follow Jesus, it would have looked quite different. Imagine if Jesus had gathered his disciples and then told them to meet with him for an hour each week, if they did not have something else to do. If that had happened, I doubt the church would have ever existed.

Jesus built relationships with his disciples by pouring his life into theirs and taking time to be with them. We cannot build strong relationships within the church without pouring our lives into one another and taking time to be together. All of the time we need to spend with our church family cannot be accomplished at the church campus. The family relationships from the church need to pour into our homes. We need to share meals together beyond communion and pot lucks. Children should play together. The men should work on projects together and teach the younger men. The women should also work on projects together and teach the younger women.

Much of what we learn in life is taught outside of formal classroom settings. When we share our lives with others, they not only learn about us, but they learn from us. Couples who have been married for a number of years can spend time with newly married couples and help model a healthy marriage for them. Couples with older children can spend time with couples with younger children and model how to raise the kids. Wisdom can be passed to others as we live our lives together.

None of these ideas are new. In fact, they are very old. Much of the learning process throughout human history has been from observing how others do things. We have made changes in the last several centuries to emphasize more structured learning, but mentors have always been and will continue to be an effective way to transmit wisdom.

By spending time with believers, people are spending time with individuals who are indwelt by the Holy Spirit. They see the way the person lives and the decisions they make. To the degree that the person is being led by the Spirit, they are modeling God's will. People encounter God through spending time with his people.

Correction (Church Discipline)

None of us are perfect. We all have moments when we fail to do the things we know we should do. All Christians are reformed rebels, and sometimes the tendency to rebel surfaces. A popular saying where I was reared is this: "You can take the boy out of the country, but you can't take the country out of the boy."

The Christian life is one that should be marked by continuous progress in sanctification. We should always strive to look more like Jesus, and we should make progress day by day. Sometimes we regress. A common term for regressing in our sanctification is "backsliding." Christians are warned not to become entangled in sin. We sometimes allow ourselves to be caught in a snare. When a believer is not living up to the expectations of God's family, the family must act.

Love is the primary motivator for correct a brother or sister struggling with sin. If our motivation is something else, we should recuse ourselves and allow another to address the situation. The goal of addressing improper behavior in the church is that the offending party would repent and restore the relationships within the church. The goal is never to exact revenge or to punish. Vengeance belongs to God.

Church discipline has two goals. The first goal is to show the seriousness of sin and the love of the congregation for the offender. Disruptive behavior in the church has to be dealt with. Sin will lead to destruction, and it cannot be ignored. A believer who is confronted with their sin has the opportunity to repent and restore their relationship with the family.

Restoration is the goal. Even when the church is forced to remove a member from the family, the removal is done with the hope that the person will repent and rejoin the family.

The second goal is to remove unregenerate people from the church family. Unfortunately, some people join churches without trusting in Jesus. While these people may be part of a local congregation they are not part of the church. When we find unregenerate church members, we should seek their salvation. However, if someone is not a genuine believer, we cannot allow them to remain in the family. In love, we must show them the seriousness of salvation, and that will mean removing them from membership. As with a regenerate (or saved) member who is removed from the church family, the hope is that they will genuinely repent, be converted, and return to the family.

People encounter God through church discipline because it shows the seriousness of sanctification and salvation. The family cannot allow sin to take root in the congregation and spoil the fellowship and worship of the body. The family also cannot allow impostors to act like they are part of the family when they are not. God corrects those he loves. As the church receives correction from God and uses that correction on itself, people will encounter God more clearly.

Personal Ministry to Believers

Ministering to other believers is a way to encounter God. People can have only a certain number of deep and meaningful relationships at a time. But the fact that we can only have deep relationships with a few people does not mean that we cannot have meaningful experiences by serving others. Personal ministry to other believers can provide an opportunity to encounter God through serving another.

Personal ministry comes in many flavors. Some people like to visit and talk with people. They may serve God's family by meeting with members who are sick, homebound, or in the hospital. Others may have people with chores at their homes or help them figure out what insurance they need to purchase. Having an outlet for the church family to care for one another is important for meeting needs within the church, but also for allowing people to come closer to God as they give of themselves in service to God.

HEALING: MINISTRY TO THE WORLD

The final purpose of the church is ministry to the world. The church ministers to the world by showing God's mercy and by evangelizing the lost. Showing God's mercy to the world means that we help meet physical and emotional needs of people. Meeting these needs can be for people inside or outside the church. Evangelism is meeting the spiritual needs of those outside the church invisible, though some of them may be members of local congregations. People encounter God through the healing ministries of the church when they have their needs met by God through his people.

Mercy

Humans have lots of needs. We are physical creatures and we have physical needs. We are also emotional creatures and we have emotional needs. Food, shelter, and companionship are but a few of the needs people have. Suffering takes place when needs go unmet, or when met the wrong way.

Becoming a believer does not make all of our needs disappear. Christians still get hungry, and need clothing, shelter, and companionship. To the best of the church family's ability, it should meet the needs of members. We should want to meet those needs, since we should have a special affection for our siblings. Paul explains how believers were zealous to meet needs of other believers: "In the midst of a very severe trial, their overflowing joy and their extreme poverty welled up in rich generosity. For I testify that they gave as much as they were able, and even beyond their ability. Entirely on their own, urgently pleaded with us for the privilege of sharing in this service to the Lord's people" (2 Cor 8:2–4). Christians have always wanted to take care of their own.

To the degree that the church family continues to have capacity to meet physical and emotional needs beyond the congregation, it should seek to meet needs in the community. Jesus directs us to show mercy, even to our enemies. "But love your enemies, do good to them, and lend to them without expecting to get anything back. Then your reward will be great, and you will be children of the Most High, because he is kind to the ungrateful and wicked. Be merciful, just as your Father is merciful" (Luke 6:35–36). Since God is merciful, we should also be merciful.

When we show mercy to people, we are acting like God. Our sanctification is progressing, and we are becoming more like Jesus. We come closer to God by showing mercy, and those who receive it encounter God's love through the dispensing of mercy by his people.

Evangelism

Humans are not only physical and emotional creatures, but also spiritual ones. As such, we have spiritual needs. Christians have had their spiritual needs met in Christ, and we have the privilege to bring spiritual healing to the world. Through evangelism, we make disciples of Jesus Christ (Matt 28:19). Local evangelism is focused in our community, and non-local evangelism (missions) is focused beyond our community.

The process of evangelism is a holistic one. The church is not told by Jesus to go into all of the nations and make converts. The church is told to make disciples. A disciple is a follower. When someone comes to faith in Jesus, he or she need to become part of a local church, where they can participate in the life of the church. Participation in the life of the church is what a disciple of Jesus Christ does. The life of the church is the tangible expression of evangelism.

People encounter God through evangelism by encountering Jesus as the gospel is presented. The more effectively we present the gospel, the more clearly God is encountered through our presentation. We should strive to present the gospel of Jesus Christ in a way that people can understand. We may have to learn new languages or new presentations so that we can help the people we are sharing with understanding the gospel message.

Chapter Seven

Encountering God by Design

GOD DESIGNED THE CHURCH FOR HUMANS TO ENCOUNTER HIM

THE CHURCH IS A special place. In a very real sense, the church is where heaven and earth meet. The church gathered is an amazing collection of human and divine in a loving embrace. God intended for the church to communicate his love to the world.

God could have used supernatural angelic beings to declare his glory to the world. God could have designated a mountain peak as the place that humans would meet with him and experience his glory. He did not choose to do those things. God chose to encounter the world through the church. The love of Jesus Christ is shared with people who need it by people who have received it.

Believers Encounter God through Each Other

The church is filled with people indwelt by the Holy Spirit and on a journey to become more like Jesus. In our daily activities, we work out our relationship with God and with others as we toil in our labors. Connections with other believers allow us to share our story and receive their stories. By spending time with believers, we develop friendship, affection, and love for them. We care for our friends and pray for their good.

As relationships with Christians grow stronger, and as we love and give of ourselves more, we are further sanctified. Jesus is seen a little more clearly as some of the grime on us is wiped away. As we are polished, so to speak, in the sanctification process, Jesus and his love are better reflected into the world. When Christians grow together, we all begin to show Jesus a little better in our lives. Those around us begin to see Jesus more clearly in our lives, and we begin to see Jesus more clearly in their lives. Ideally, fully sanctified believers would reflect Jesus like a room of mirrors with Jesus standing in the middle. Everywhere you look, you would see Jesus reflected. The church should be like that. Unfortunately, many of us need a good cleaning. Our ability to reflect Jesus is diminished by our sin and selfishness. Through the ministries of the church, our dirty and damaged mirrors are cleaned, repaired, and polished.

The church is the place where we go to encounter God because it is the place where those who image God and reflect his glory gather. Although all humans image God, only those who have trusted in Jesus intentionally reflect him. Humanity is in rebellion against God and, to continue with the mirror analogy, is turned away from God. Rebellious humanity reflects the world, not God. When we turn back toward God in repentance, we are oriented properly, and then we just need to be cleaned and repaired so that our reflection will become clearer. The church is the place where we are aligned the right way, cleaned, and repaired.

The church is not just a place where someone comes to get instructions on how to live and how to encounter God. Christians live and encounter God together through the church.

Nonbelievers Encounter God through His Church

People who are not part of the church encounter God by encountering his people. God is present to all of his creation, but often people do not notice or care to see him. The creation is singing praise and glory to God at all times. Unfortunately, the beautiful song of creation has become white noise to those who have turned away from the Creator. It is difficult to begin to pay attention to something you have dismissed as irrelevant, or worse, hostile.

Those who choose to pay attention to creation's song often misinterpret it. General revelation tells us some things about God, but the information it reveals can be wrongly applied to false gods. The creation itself can become an object of worship, and the greatness it proclaims can be applied to itself.

God can directly confront his creatures who are living in rebellion, and he sometimes does. Reports abound of people who have dreamed of God or who encountered God through mystical experiences. The most typical way that God confronts people, however, is through his church. The church is a mobilized indwelt family extending God's kingdom into the world.

People in rebellion against God meet him in a stranger who gives directions or who frequents their business. Christians have God with them when they meet those who have shunned God and turned away from his love. Without even recognizing it, the world is encountering God through the lives of every follower of Jesus Christ. God is blessing people and exposing sin and selfishness through his church. He is bringing salt and light into the dark and rotting corners of the world with the lives of his adopted children. If people want to encounter God, they need to be around his people.

EXISTENTIAL NEEDS ARE BEST MET IN THE CHURCH

Earlier I laid out several existential needs humans have. I categorized them as needs related to human autonomy and human dependence. The needs humans have can be met in various ways, some healthy and others destructive. Within the family structure of the church, people can have their needs of autonomy and dependence met. God designed the church, and we are not surprised that what we need to thrive, as humans can be found in the place that God designed for us to operate.

Needs of Autonomy Are Met in the Church

The church is a special type of community. In the church, God provides people with the opportunity to have intimate connections with one another. He also allows people to make decisions, find their calling, and do things that have long-lasting, even eternal, effects. The church should function like a family, but even within family structures, people are individuals who have to make their own decisions and forge a way for themselves within the larger group.

Need for Self-Direction

The need for self-direction, which is the ability to make decisions for oneself, is beautifully expressed within the life of the church. The first example of this is becoming a part of the church itself. Although many people are born into families that are part of the church, each person must come to a point in their lives where they repent of their own sin and turn to Jesus for salvation. While parents can pray for their children and teach them the great doctrines and heritage of the Christian faith, they cannot choose for the child. Those who come to faith in Jesus do so as individuals. Individuals who make up God's family are the church.

After becoming part of the family, there are many more decisions we have to make. Each person has to progress along the path of sanctification, and all of our routes are different. Every day we have to make decisions about how we will spend the day and how our lives will reflect Jesus. Sometimes we make good choices, and other times we fail. We have only ourselves to blame for the choices we make about the way we will live our lives. We do not have control over everything that comes into our lives, but we do choose how we will respond. Our responses are themselves conditioned on the previous choices we have made about how we will live. We choose how we will live each day. We choose how we will honor God or how we will disobey. We choose to be distracted or to be focused. The choices are not always easy, and beyond our own will there are external factors that push and pull us in all kinds of directions.

Within the life of the church, we choose how involved we will be in our spiritual growth. We choose to study, pray, and serve those in need, or we choose not to do these things. When the call goes out to a congregation that a member's family has lost their house to a fire, we are left with a choice of whether or not to assist them. When a couple has a baby and the church organizes a group of people to bring food to the new family, we choose whether or not to participate. We are not alone in these choices. God leads us by using our friends in the church. God may have our friends encourage us to step out into a new or challenging arena. God may have our friends caution us before we make decisions that may be foolish or dangerous.

Need for Significance

One of the great benefits of being a part of the church is having our needs for significance met. The first way that this need is met in the church is, like the need for self-direction, by becoming part of the church. If a purpose of humanity is to glorify God by being in a loving relationship with him, then becoming a part of Jesus' church is a significant action. When we become part of the church, we are becoming, in part, what we were created to be by God. Becoming part of the church is significant because it is part of God's design, not because of our feelings about it.

Often people search for significance, and they construct the criteria by which they will determine what is significant or not. When I was younger, I felt that I would have a degree of significance if I was able to attend concerts of certain musicians and groups. I listened to their music and purchased it (on cassette tape or CD). I purchased shirts with their name and logo. As a fan, I felt that attending one of their concerts would be a monumental and significant event in my life. When I did go to a concert, I had a sense of significance. Many years later, I realized that the significance I attached to those types of events had changed. I appreciated the experiences, but the significance of having attended concerts was eclipsed by a new perspective in life and new life events.

Being part of the church, however, is something we were designed for, and we are not all that we can be when that part of our life is lacking. A car may function to some degree without an engine, but cars are designed to have engines. Only when a car has an engine can it function the way it was designed. Becoming part of the church meets the need for significance because the decision to become part of the church has everlasting consequence.

Apart from joining the church, other actions within the church also offer needs of significance to be met. Passing along the faith to others is tremendously significant. Whether we are teaching others how to live as Christians or sharing the gospel so that people have an opportunity to become Christians, the actions are meaningful. By teaching the faith to others, they are empowered to serve and make progress in sanctification. Evangelism is the process by which lives are changed and people become part of God's family. The effect of teaching in the church is very significant.

Other types of service are also meaningful and significant. Meeting the physical needs of members of the church is a tangible way that God's love is experienced and expressed. Alleviating suffering is not inconsequential.

We see people who are not Christians seeking to improve people's lives because they see it as making a difference in the world. They are correct, but in the church the difference is that we understand that the effect lasts far longer than this life.

The choices individuals make to become part of the church, to serve, and to share the gospel have effects that will reverberate for all time. Serving Christ in his church is by no means a menial or insignificant choice. Generations of people have been affected by those who served before, and more will be affected by those who serve now and in the future. The significance of those actions will be on display for all time. There is no better way to have significance than to serve God in his church.

Need for Real Choices

Participation in the local church allows believers the opportunity to make choices about how they will live their lives and how they will participate in the community of faith. Church participation is not compulsory; people have to decide to become part of the church. They must also continue to uphold the community standards within the church if they wish to remain a part of the body. While there is to some degree a large decision regarding association with the church or not, there are a multitude of other, less momentous decisions believers have to make on a routine basis.

Christians choose to participate in the worship of God in their local congregations. They choose to pray to God for blessing or confession of sin. They choose if they are going to participate in the life of the church through ministry and fellowship with one another. Many times each day, a believer is confronted with situations that call for him or her to choose how they will behave. The decision to pray, tithe, serve, comfort, or worship is constantly thrust in front of a Christian, and a choice has to be made. Choices belong to the individual because they are responsible for participating in the church family. Although friends and family can provide guidance and encouragement, individuals must decide what they are going to do.

The choices Christians make propel them in the direction of sanctification or steer them away from Jesus. Choosing to pray with and comfort a friend who has suffered a loss helps to conform the Christian toward a more complete sanctification. In other words, he or she becomes more Christlike. Failing to help that friend does not make the Christian more sanctified. Choosing to violate God's commands contributes to a reversal of the process of sanctification; it makes the believer less Christlike.

Many of the teachings of Christianity are centered around guidance for the choices believers face. Christians discuss how to make the choices that they may face within the context of their faith. They also discuss decisions they have made and how they came to those decisions.

Decisions within the church are both real and have consequence. The life of the church provides an environment where the Christian has opportunity to make significant decisions and to discuss those decisions with others who can provide wise counsel. Those decisions can be lived out within the body of the church, and the effects of those choices can be seen within the life of the church. The opportunity to make real choices is available within the church family.

Needs of Human Dependence Met in the Church

Human needs for autonomy have been shown to be met within the proper function of the church. Now we turn our attention to examine how human needs for dependence are met within the church. To some extent, this is an easier task than the former. The church is a collection of people who are joined together with a common faith in Jesus Christ. Nevertheless, a clear statement of the needs examined earlier in this work deserves a clear discussion of how they are met within the functioning of the church.

Need for Temporal Security and Transcendent Security

The church is a community that should function like a family. The family is an institution that provides protection and inclusion for its members. The church is an excellent place to find temporal and transcendent security.

The early church modeled caring for one another. In the early chapters of Acts, the church is seen sharing possessions. Those who have given up everything to follow Jesus are cared for by the larger church body (Acts 2:44). The theme of caring for one another is not lost in the New Testament. Paul made a financial collection during his ministry to aid the church in Jerusalem. Other writers address the issue of meeting physical and emotional needs within the church as well.

> This is how we know what love is: Jesus Christ laid down his life for us. And we ought to lay down our lives for our brothers and sisters. If anyone has material possessions and sees a brother or sister in need but has no pity on them, how can the love of God be in that person? Dear children, let us not love with words or speech but with actions and in truth. (1 John 3:16–18)

The fledgling church made caring for one another a priority. One of the reasons that they cared for each other so well was that the sacrifice to become part of the church was often very severe. Jesus called his followers to become part of his new community at the expense of their own families. The strong bond in the ancient Mediterranean family is foreign to most Westerners, but the consequences of leaving your family could mean leaving most, if not all, of your material possessions and being rejected and shunned by your blood relatives. The decision to become part of Jesus' new group had significant social and financial consequences for many believers. The only way the church could survive was to care for one another. Tertullian, an early church leader, wrote about the way the church cared for her own. He contrasted the behavior of Christians with the pagans of his day.

> On the monthly day, if he likes, each puts in a small donation; but only if it be his pleasure, and only if he be able: for there is no compulsion; all is voluntary. These gifts are, as it were, piety's deposit fund. For they are not taken thence and spent on feasts, and drinking-bouts, and eating-houses, but to support and bury poor people, to supply the wants of boys and girls destitute of means and parents, and of old persons confined now to the house; such, too, as have suffered shipwreck; and if there happen to be any in the mines, or banished to the islands, or shut up in the prisons, for nothing but their fidelity to the cause of God's church, they become the nurslings of their confession. But it is mainly the deeds of a love so noble that lead many to put a brand upon us. See, they say, how they love one another, for themselves are animated by mutual hatred; how they are ready even to die for one another, for they themselves will sooner put to death. (Tertullian, *Apol.* 39)

The church met the physical and emotional needs of its members, because in most cases, the church was the only place that those believers had left. The church still meets the needs of its own. Churches provide for the poor and will often care for their own who have need. Beyond physical needs, the church also provides relationships for people to share their lives and to discuss difficult and painful issues.

Transcendent needs are also met within the church. The church is the place where the followers of Jesus meet. Christian teaching understands that only through the atoning work of Christ is any hope of a proper relationship with God possible. The Christian view of salvation is rooted in the person and work of Jesus Christ, and is guaranteed by his resurrection. For the Christian, security beyond this life can only be attained in Christ, and to be in Christ is to be in the church. Transcendent security is not only met within the church, but it is met exclusively in the church. Other attempts to find transcendent security are doomed to fail.

Outside of the church, there is no salvation. A strong claim, no doubt, but a claim that the church has held to since her inception. Jesus made a distinction between those who desired to retain allegiance to identity in Abraham and those who followed him. Those who trusted in their position in Abraham were actually children of the devil.

> Jesus said to them, "If God were your Father, you would love me, for I have come here from God. I have not come on my own; God sent me. Why is my language not clear to you? Because you are unable to hear what I say. You belong to your father, the devil, and you want to carry out your father's desires. He was a murderer from the beginning, not holding to the truth, for there is no truth in him. When he lies, he speaks his native language, for he is a liar and the father of lies. Yet because I tell the truth, you do not believe me! Can any of you prove me guilty of sin? If I am telling the truth, why don't you believe me? Whoever belongs to God hears what God says. The reason you do not hear is that you do not belong to God." (John 8:42–47)

The decision to reject Jesus, even for those who were part of God's people chosen in Abraham, was considered by Jesus to show that they were children of the devil.

The exclusive nature of the call to follow Jesus was understood by the early church and by subsequent generations of Christians who understood Christianity as the only hope for people beyond this life. If Christianity is true, and if Christians are right to claim exclusive hope beyond this life, then not only is the church the place to find transcendent security, it is the only place to find it. In this case, the church is the only place where the human need for transcendent security can be met.

Need for Love

> A new command I give you: Love one another. As I have loved you, so you must love one another. By this everyone will know that you are my disciples, if you love one another. (John 13:34–35)

One of the ways the people will know Christians is by their love for each other. The concept of identification by love for the church is rooted in the Gospels. Love for Christian brothers and sisters should clearly identify followers of Jesus.

Tangible expressions of caring for one another, or acts of love, were examined above. Loving relationships can be found within the church. The primary way of identifying one another for the early church, and in many churches today, is with the designation of a sibling title. Christians have called one another brother and sister from the earliest times. Jesus even identified with his followers in contrast to his natural family (see Mark 3 and Matthew 12).

Whether or not someone has natural siblings, the closeness and love of sibling relationships can be found in the church. Since sibling relationships mirror strong friendships, we can say that relationships that are able to fill the role of both siblings and friendships are available to those who are part of the church. In addition, many people have found their future spouse within the church as well. The point is that numerous relationships that allow people to experience love are available within the body of Christ.

Love from God is also available in the church. The church is the place where God gathers those he loves. By being in the church, people are reconciled with God and encounter him as a loving father. Outside of the church, the best that one could hope for is to relate to God as a benevolent Creator. Inside the church, the full spectrum of God's love is available, including intimacy, instruction, and chastisement.

Need for Acceptance, Affirmation, and Connection

Humans have always drawn lines of separation. Differences in tribe and tongue have led to violence and distrust. Sometimes acceptance in a group is restricted to birth, with admission though other means as difficult or impossible. Other times, shared beliefs are the gateway to group affiliation. The church is a place where people are able to find acceptance based on their relationship to Jesus Christ.

Across the landscape of Christianity, many types of congregations abound. Some congregations have very little diversity within, and others are a mosaic of cultures and races. The church, when functioning as it should, is a place where one is accepted not based on what we have done but based on what Jesus has done for us. People in the church have to have a relationship with Christ; that is to say, they should themselves be followers of Jesus, but apart from that there is no need to have other types of similarities.

Sometimes the church is described as a group of people who have nothing else in common except Jesus. There is truth to that statement, but I think it needs to be explained. Perhaps a better way to state the point would be to say the only thing that people in the church have to have in common is Jesus. We can have many things in common with one another and be part of the church. One thing local congregations will have in common is their geographical location. But the only thing that one must have to be in the universal church is a relationship with Jesus Christ.

Local congregations, however, are not the universal church and will have other requirements for membership. Some of those requirements will be stated, and others will be implicit. Joining a local congregation will necessitate that a person has certain other things in common with the membership than simply just a relationship with Jesus. Acceptance in the universal church requires only a relationship with Jesus, and local churches should be careful not to place more barriers than necessary for acceptance into their local congregations. People can and do find acceptance in local churches. Despite all of the issues that divide, the church accepts people and gives them a place to belong. Without a doubt, the church is a place where people can find acceptance.

Affirmation and encouragement are also found inside of the church. Christianity is a faith that calls for change. Although the basis for our relationship with God has been accomplished by Christ, we are not to remain unchanged. God desires for us to grow in our salvation, or to become more sanctified. Jesus loved us while we were sinners and died for us so we could have a relationship with him. He loves us too much to let us remain conformed to this world.

The church celebrates and affirms the milestones of the Christian faith. Coming to faith in Christ is proclaimed to the creation by baptism, which is encouraged and celebrated by the church. As we become more and more like Christ, we are encouraged through the life of the church. Regular proclamation of God's word should not only affirm our faith, it should encourage us to be more faithful. Teaching ministries should not only reinforce the foundations of our common creed, they should prompt us to know more about God. Serving in the church should not only provide a tangible expression of our commitment to Jesus, it should be used to foster a deeper desire to please God.

In all aspects of church life, members are there to come alongside one another for support, affirmation, and encouragement. Since everyone is on a similar path, struggles will often be similar. The encouragement and affirmation will come from people who understand the types of issues others face. Many of them will have struggled or will be struggling with similar issues. Even though everyone is different, many of our struggles and issues are the same—they are just dressed in different clothes.

Young couples trying to figure out how to live with their spouse or how to adapt to children in the home is not unique. Couples have dealt with this from time immemorial. Financial stress or insecurity about a job or business are common to people in and out of the church. Difficulties with parents or siblings are also to be found in all walks of life. The church is no different. The difference in the church will be some of the ways that we encourage people to work through these issues. Christians have walked through all kinds of difficulties. The church is filled with people who have been through just about everything under the sun. People can find many others who have shared struggles in the church.

Need for Justice and Order

The cry for justice has echoed through the centuries and continues to this day. Those living under the boot of oppression shout petitions toward the halls of heaven, begging for relief and for wrongs to be set right. Do those calls fall on deaf ears? Is there anyone able to hear the voices? Is anyone able to make right the wrongs?

The way people answer these questions are basic to the way they view the world itself. The atheist and certain other religions have to say that humans are the only option for hearing the cries and setting things right. Only by pulling ourselves up by our own bootstraps can we hope to have a semblance of justice. Christians have another answer.

While the best that an atheist can hope for is to correct present and future wrongs, the Christian can have assurance that everything will be set right by a just and all-powerful God. The child, abused and tortured even before it could speak, will have justice because God knows what happened and will see justice done. The families slaughtered by marauding tribes or mercenaries, whose life was cut short without warning, will have a just judge adjudicating the case. No evidence will be lost. No favors will be bought. Justice will be served. The God of Christianity is concerned with justice and is able to mete it out. He is, after all, the basis for justice, and his word and character are its foundations. No deed will escape his eye; his judgments will be true and just.

The faith of the church provides a coherent view of God and an ultimate view of justice fulfilled in the eschaton. Beyond a simple hope in a future judgment, the church also provides an opportunity for people to work toward temporal justice. God can use and has used his people to right wrongs in the world. The American experience finds Christians working to end slavery and to promote equality among humans. The basis for valuing all of humanity is rooted in the Christian doctrine that humans are made in the image of God. The church has participated and will continue to participate in bringing justice to the world.

Aside from justice, order within the universe is also explained by God who brings order to chaos. Questions about why anything exists at all and why the things that do exist seem to be fine-tuned for life are answered by the faith held by the church. The Christian conception of God supervening over the universe as a just judge provides a sufficient ground for the conception of justice and order and a reason to see needs for such conceptions met.

ENCOUNTERING GOD IS NOT PRIMARILY A MYSTICAL EXPERIENCE

Spiritual experiences, when portrayed in modern media, are fantastic and resemble the special effects of top tier movies. Fascination with fog machines, lighting, and grand imagery fill the empty space left by descriptions of encounters with God. A common visual technique for portraying a spiritual encounter is to flood the camera view with a blinding light. Encounters portrayed in movies, whether they are religious or not, often have these types of elements. When movie characters encounter things that are beyond this world (spiritual or alien), smoke and lights often accompany the characters in their scene.

A danger in consuming stories that use smoke, fog, and special lighting as cues that a character is in some sense touching an alien realm is that the effects themselves can be expected and treated as evidence of the encounter rather than a pointer to the fact the encounter is taking place. Because we consume so much popular media and because storytelling is an effective way to teach, many have assumed that encounters with the divine should have elements found in movies. When someone is searching for God, we expect to see a smoky area that we need to walk in.

Some churches and other religious events take advantage of special-effect technology to make their meeting space meet these artificial expectations we have been taught to expect by Hollywood. Churches have purchased smoke machines and theatrical lighting. Sometimes entering into a room for a congregational service resembles entering a theater for a production. While I think it is wise to engage all of the senses in worship, it can be overdone. While effects like lighting, smoke, and sound can enhance and prepare people to encounter God, they can also be used as a replacement for the encounter.

Some may counter and say that there are examples of light, smoke, and sound when people come into contact with God, and we have those examples in the Bible itself. I agree. There are descriptions of God which include smoke and light. There are examples where people encountering God hear sounds. The point is not that these things never happen, but that they are rare occurrences and cannot be a prerequisite for a genuine encounter with God.

God Works through His People Primarily

The most common way God interacts with humans is through his people. The Bible is filled with examples of God communicating to people by using his own people. There are times that God spoke to people without using other humans, but often God chooses not to communicate that way. God communed in the garden with Adam and Eve, walked with Enoch, instructed Noah to build an ark, wrestled with Jacob, visited Abraham, led Israel through the wilderness, spoke to Moses on the mountain, whispered to Samuel in the night, affirmed Jesus at his baptism, told Peter to eat previously unclean animals, and whisked John away in his apocalypse. These examples, however exiting and epic, are rare examples of God's action.

Most often we see God working through his people. God used Joseph to interpret the dreams of the Pharaoh and eventually provide for his people in the famine. Moses was God's mouthpiece to both the nation of Israel and Egypt. Various judges led Israel in times of crisis. Boaz showed God's lovingkindness to Naomi. A prophet declared the fate of Eli's house. Samuel anointed kings for Israel. Nathan rebuked David for his sin. Elijah and Elisha declared the word of the Lord to Israel. Esther spoke to the king on behalf of Israel. Other Old Testament prophets corrected and rebuked Israel and her neighbors. The New Testament is filled with God working through his people.

The pattern we see is that God commonly uses his people to bless, rebuke, and proclaim his word. While God does not only use his people, he sometimes uses angelic beings or directly communicates with individuals, by far the most common way for God to communicate is through his people. Interestingly, God tended to speak directly to people in the early books of the Bible. Before the nation of Israel is established in the holy land, it was more common for God to communicate directly with biblical figures. After the establishment of Israel in the holy land, God's communication is more commonly to prophets who communicate his message to the people. With the establishment of the church and the indwelling of the Holy Spirit, nearly all communication from God is mediated through Christians.

God Uses the church to Encounter the World

Since the common way of God communicating to humanity is through the use of his people, and the ultimate expression of God's people is the church, the church is the primary way God communicates his will to the world. Life in the church is not only the place where humanity finds its proper expression and fulfillment, it is God's mouthpiece to the world.

From the beginning of the church in Jerusalem, God has been using his people to share the gospel and make known his will. The church has spoken God's word to herself and the culture around her. The effects of God using his people to communicate his will to the world has been unimaginable. The church began with the Jewish scriptures, the Old Testament, and the teachings of Jesus as her guide. From that foundation, God produced additional Scriptures, the New Testament. Christians have engaged their culture and captured it for the glory of God.

The Church Speaking Internally

The church, at its inception, did not have the intellectual traditions and theological refinement that the modern church has. It took millennia of internal conversation and exposure to God's word to have a better grasp of our theology. The study of God and his interaction with the world is no easy task, especially when categories that we take for granted were not even conceived of at the beginning.

Over time, the church worked out difficult questions of the nature of God and the divinity of Christ. These discussions were not always easy, and the answers to the questions that were raised were not always immediately clear. The church wrestled with heresy as people attempted to understand God's word within the community of the church. Discussions of the nature of Christ and the Trinity were early issues that caused much controversy. Even today, many Christians have deficient views of these topics, and we can imagine the difficulty early Christians had when discussing these issues. We have reasonably well-thought-out philosophical and theological categories to work with. The early church did not. The concept of a person, taken for granted in both theological and philosophical circles today, came out of the discussion of the Trinity, as the church struggled to define what they believed God's word taught.

The continual speaking of God's word within the church has led to changes to the way the church conceives of herself and the world. Sometimes those changes have led to violence inside of the church and violence directed outside of the church. Speaking God's word to one another has led to great works of theology, philosophy, art, and architecture. It has also led to reformation and division.

As the church continues to speak God's word to herself, we can hope that God will use it to better inform our beliefs and bring unity among his people. We should pray for unity, regardless of what that will look like. Jesus himself prayed that his followers would be united. Continued confrontation of God's word with his people should make the followers of Christ more clearly reflect his image.

The Church Speaking Externally

The church has also spoken the word of God beyond the boundaries of the church. The church had to do this to expand and continue to grow. Since the inception of the church the message of Jesus has confronted those who were not his followers and was used to bring people into the church. Each new member of the church had to have God's word presented to him or her in one form or another.

The early church grew and soon found persecution from Jewish and Roman quarters. Persecution only fueled the fire of the gospel, and the church continued to grow in spite of the difficulties she faced. The church did something that would have been thought to be inconceivable in the ancient world: it conquered Rome. The Roman Empire was the undisputed power in its region, and at times waged war against Christians. The unlikely acceptance of Christianity within the empire and the eventual rise of Christianity to dominate the Romans would have been too fantastic to believe when early Christians were scattered from Jerusalem.

Christians continued to confront the world with the word of God. They spoke God's words with their lips and their lives. God's word is powerful and accomplishes what he intends. Even the mighty Roman Empire was not able to stand against it. The church has continued to engage the world with the Word of God and the church has grown, against all odds. The church is continuing to press into the outermost places of the Earth with God's word. Evangelism and missions are the natural outworking of God's people encountering the world on God's behalf. The church will continue to speak God's word to the world until God's purposes are accomplished.

Proclamation is the Job of the Church

God has chosen his people to be his mouthpiece to the world. He could use other means to spread the gospel, as he can speak directly to humans. He could do this by speaking with individuals, like he did with Samuel. God is able to speak with anyone at any time; nothing limits God from communicating the gospel in this way. God could also appear to masses of people, like he did when leading the Israelites in the wilderness. He could use angelic beings to be his mouthpiece. Legions of angels could be dispatched to speak with individuals, like Gabriel did with Mary, or angels could carry trumpets across the sky to proclaim the gospel of Jesus Christ. Nothing prevents God from doing this. It seems that God has chosen not to proclaim his word in this manner.

God could also use the natural world to be his mouthpiece. The gospel could be proclaimed in the stars, clouds, waters, or from the mouths of animals. God has used the natural world in the past and has caused animals to speak in the past. God could do something similar to what he has done in the past if he chose to do so; nothing prevents God from doing this. Again, God has chosen not to proclaim his word this way.

The church is who God has chosen to be his mouthpiece. The church is specifically told to proclaim the gospel and to baptize and teach others. We may wonder why God would choose to proclaim his word in this manner. We may think that there are better methods to get the word out. Whatever we may think of God's choice, we must understand that the church is his chosen method. If we are part of the church, we have the responsibility to speak God's word to the world. Our responsibility is to proclaim God's word with our lips and our lives.

Living and Loving One Another is Evidence of God to the World

Jesus told his disciples that the world would know that they followed him if they loved one another. As Christians, our lives should be a witness to the world. Specifically, our lives will let others know we follow Jesus when we love other Christians. In the world of the Bible, family connections were very important. Christians lived together and treated one another as if they were siblings, which meant that they cared deeply for one another. They would help each other and think of the good of others before themselves.

The way they lived, specifically the love they had for one another, allowed people to see the difference between the Christian community and the rest of the world. The church today should learn from the early church and model love for one another. Christian love should be a distinctive mark of being part of the church. When Christians love one another and demonstrate that love with their lives, the verbal witness will be taken more seriously. Our lives should illustrate what our lips profess. The world around us will have difficulty ignoring the gospel when the lives of its bearers show love for one another.

Mercy and Grace (Blessings) are Distributed by the Church

Since God has chosen to encounter the world thought his people, the world will be blessed through the church. God identified the church as the fount of his mercy and grace. God has and will bless the world through Abraham as promised, and the church is the place from which that blessing flows.

The church is where people can find the message of salvation. The only hope for humans is to have a restored relationship with God. This only happens by the grace of God. The grace of God for humans is tied up in the gospel of Jesus Christ. The church allows the world to be blessed by sharing the gospel with the world. As sinners come to repentance and faith in Christ, not only does the church grow, but the blessings of God are poured out on the world. As the church grows, not only do more and more people experience the blessings of God's grace, but more and more vessels of his grace and mercy go forth. The blessings of salvation are carried forth by the church as she encounters the world with God's word.

The church is also the place where people are able to have fulfillment. As presented previously, the church is the place where humanity is able to function properly. Our needs can be met in the church. We are able to have all the relationships we need to live a full life within the church. The blessing of living a full life as a human is available through the church.

The church is the place where the knowledge of God and his will are located. There are two thousand years of refining conversations about the church's theology and practice. Knowledge of how to be the church resides in the church, along with knowledge of God and his plans. The blessings of knowledge are available through the church.

The church is the place where peace with God and one another is found. When the church functions as she should, peace will abound. As the church grows and confronts a world at war with God, the blessings of peace are dispensed by the church. Reconciliation to God and the peace this brings with God will be the beginning to the end of all war. As God encounters the world through the church, the blessings of peace pour out on the world.

SEARCHING FOR GOD ELSEWHERE

Throughout this work, I have tried to present a case for the ability of humans to encounter God and have their needs met. I have argued that God designed humans and created the world such that humans could encounter him. I have argued that human needs are real and are best met within the church.

Not everyone is a Christian, however, and many people search for God apart from the church. Even some who claim to follow Jesus do not identify with the church. Some people deny that God exists and see no need to search for something that they do not believe exists.

What can we say about attempts to encounter God apart from the church? To answer this, we must approach it from three different perspectives. First, we will examine the perspective person who claims to follow Jesus but wants to do that apart from the church. Second, we will examine the perspective of the person who desires to encounter God but chooses to search for God apart from Christianity. Third, we will examine the perspective of the person who does not believe there is a God to encounter.

The Christian Without the Church

The Christian who lives without the church is missing out on tremendous blessings that God has provided and fail to encounter him as they could. Humans are designed to be in a community like the church. Looking for the opportunity to make close relationships in organizations other than the church is filled with potential pitfalls and lacks the support structure the church is designed to provide.

Christians can and should make friends with people who are not believers. Friendships with non-believers can be healthy and valuable. Since non-believing friends will not have the same goals and religious commitments, however, they will be unable to provide encouragement aligned with distinctly Christian teaching. While it is true that much of Western society has been influenced by Christianity and many of the values Christ taught have become part of the fabric of Western thought, much Christian wisdom remains decidedly outside of popular culture. Friendships that have a part of their basis in the shared community of the church can tap into the parts of the Christian tradition that have been ignored or rejected by popular society.

The church also provides opportunities for leadership and risk-taking within a safe environment. Non-religious groups may also provide opportunities, but secular values and goals are often contrary to the sanctification process. Individual growth can and does take place apart from the church, but the church has built-in boundaries to keep people focused on growing in their faith as well as building skills.

Additional reasons include a lack of opportunity to perform the functions of the church properly. Worship as an individual, apart from the church, is lesser than worshiping God with his people. It can be done, and it can be meaningful, however, it should not be done with the exclusion of corporate worship. The same is true for teaching/learning. I can learn alone, but I lose the insights of other Christians when I do so. Fellowship with Christians outside of a church setting can be done, but it lacks dimensions of relationships that come with mutual accountability. Merciful activities and Evangelism can be done apart from a church, but again, doing those activities either alone or with people who lack the accountability found in the church, lack opportunities for deeper growth.

It makes little sense that followers of Christ would exclude themselves from the community that Jesus died for. Christians should be involved in local churches. Any spirituality or growth that an individual may have in isolation from the church is lesser than what could be produced within the church. Christians need the church if they are to reach their full potential.

The Religious Person Without the Church

Religious people who are not Christians miss many blessings from God and fail to encounter him properly. While they may have some similar opportunities that Christians have in their religious traditions, the main problem is that they lack the opportunity to have a saving relationship with God. Even if they could have all of the benefits of community, they have no transcendent security. Judgment will come to them in the end.

Since Christianity teaches that the only way to have peace with God is through the sacrifice Jesus made, other traditions/religions are unable to have peace with God. Many people reject the idea that the exclusive nature of Christianity is true. Many people claim that God is accessible through any number of religions. Christianity that is faithful to the traditions handed down must affirm that Jesus made exclusive claims to be the only way to God. The church believed his claims and passed them down through the years. The question that has to be considered is whether or not the claims of Christian exclusivity are true.

Religious people who follow traditions other than Christianity have to decide if the claims of Christ and his church are true or not. If they conclude that the claims are true, then the only reasonable course of action is to become a follower of Jesus. If they conclude that the claims are false, then the reasonable course of action would be to follow whichever claims to truth that they believe to be true. From the perspective of a Christian, however, religious people who are not Christians need Christ as their savior. In other words, they need to become Christians.

The Atheist Without the Church

Atheists miss many blessings from God and fail to encounter him properly. Fulfillment that can be found in a materialistic view of the world will, for obvious reasons, neglect to meet spiritual needs. Those needs are real, however, and will still need to be met. Humans often try to meet needs with methods that are not well-suited. Emotional needs are sometimes masked by alcohol or other substances. Needs to connect with people on deep emotional levels can sometimes be filled with obsessive behaviors. While anyone, regardless of religious affiliation, can try to meet needs with something that will only mask the need, atheists lack the ability to meet spiritual needs. Denying that there is such a need may help some cope, but if the needs are real, then they go unmet for the atheist. The atheist does not seek to encounter God, so they will not encounter him properly. From the perspective of the Christian, however, atheists need to encounter God, and they need Christ as their Savior. Atheists, just like everyone else, need to become Christians.

GOING FORWARD

My hope is that you have been encouraged by this work. If you are a Christian, I hope this will provide you with ways to think about the value of our faith and the church that will strengthen your faith. The church is the way that God encounters the world (most of the time). We, as part of the church, have a responsibility to engage the world as representatives of God. I pray that you will grow deeper in your relationship with God and with the church. May the grace of the Lord Jesus Christ, and the love of God, and the fellowship of the Holy Spirit be with you all (2 Cor 13:14).

Bibliography

Erickson, Millard J. *Christian Theology*. 2nd ed. Grand Rapids: Baker Academic, 1998.
Grenz, Stanley J. *Theology for the Community of God*. Grand Rapids: Eerdmans, 2000.
Hellerman, Joseph H. *When the Church Was a Family: Recapturing Jesus' Vision for Authentic Christian Community*. Nashville: B. & H. Academic, 2009.
New World Encyclopedia. "Johannes Kepler." http://www.newworldencyclopedia.org/entry/Johannes_Kepler.
Osborn, Larry. *Sticky Church*. Grand Rapids: Zondervan, 2008.
Williams, Clifford. *Existential Reasons for Belief in God: A Defense of Desires and Emotions for Faith*. Downers Grove: InterVarsity, 2011.

www.ingramcontent.com/pod-product-compliance
Lightning Source LLC
Chambersburg PA
CBHW071505150426
43191CB00009B/1421